D1606479

# CHILDREN
## OF THE
# DAWN
## VISIONS
### OF THE
## NEW FAMILY

Also by the Author


Live Your Health
The Art and Practice of Holistic Healing
Reuben and Joshua Halpern
Ross Books 1980

# CHILDREN
## OF THE
# DAWN
## VISIONS
### OF THE
## NEW FAMILY

# JOSHUA HALPERN

ONLY WITH LOVE
PUBLICATIONS
1986

Children of the Dawn
Visions of the New Family


Published By

ONLY WITH LOVE
PUBLICATIONS
P.O. Box 5
Bodega, California 94922


Book & Art Design ©1986 Joshua Halpern
Cover Design Joshua Halpern
and Tamara Slayton

Joshua Halpern                                    Library of Congress in Publication Data
    Children of the Dawn
        1. Family        2. Child Development        3. Birthing & Bonding
        I. Halpern, Joshua

ISBN 0-9613143-7-0

PRINTED IN THE UNITED STATES OF AMERICA

# TABLE OF CONTENTS

## BOOK ONE:
## PROCREATION

## BOOK TWO:
## INITIATION

# BOOK THREE:
# MATURATION

# INVOCATION

My nation, behold it in kindness!

A sacred praise I am making
A sacred praise I am making

The day of the sun has been my strength
The path of the moon shall be my robe

A sacred praise I am making
A sacred praise I am making

Black Elk

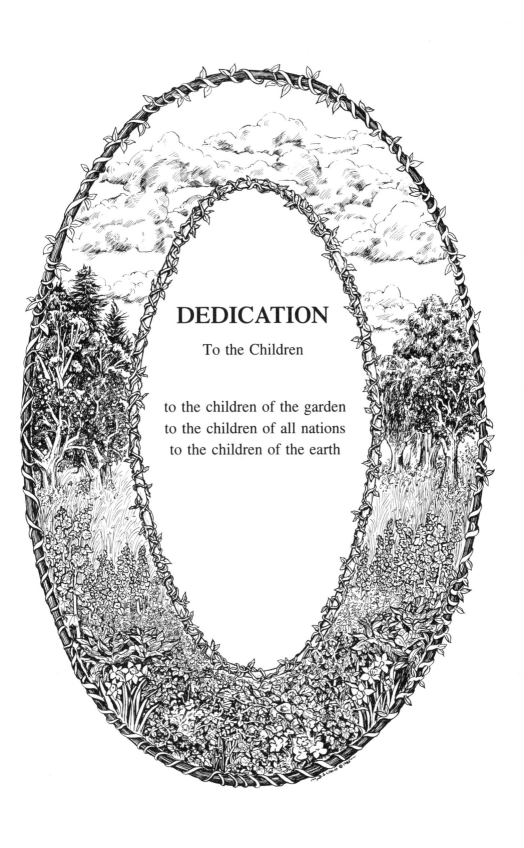

# DEDICATION

To the Children

to the children of the garden
to the children of all nations
to the children of the earth

to the children of seekers, ex-slaves and immigrants
to the children of the native born
to the children of workers
to the children of cleaners and cooks
to the children of farmers and peasants
to the children of soldiers
to the children of broken homes
to the children of the night who continue to roam
to the children of street walkers
to the children of the morning star
to the children of the dawn
to the children of dancers, singers, and saxophonists
to the children of poets and story-tellers
to the children of public servants
to the children of the four corners
to the children of all directions
to the children of the canyons
to the children of the shores
to the children of the alley ways
to the children left to cry
to the children who will have the courage when the time comes
to the children of mystics
to the children of single-mothers
to the children of the underground railroad
to the children of freedom marchers
to the children of the naked, nameless and homeless
to the children of meditators and yogis
to the children of freedom fighters and shamans
to the children of exiles
to the children of assassinated prophets
to the children of living minstrels
to the children of the choir
to the children of whirling dervishes

to You, dearest one. You brought me across the waters
    to these glorious shores
may I return a million times more to be in your Presence.

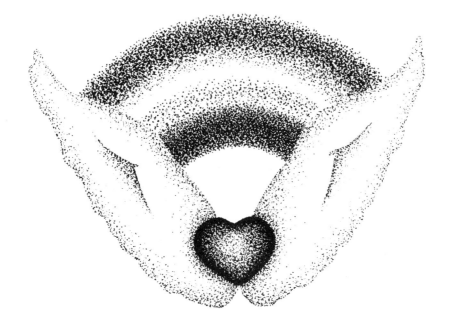

# INTRODUCTION

## Flying on the Wings of the One-Heart

The Tree of Life is Flowering. These are the First Days of a new cycle in Creation. The Phoenix has arisen from the ash. When the Dawn comes everything changes. Nations and gene pools transform. Thought waves and vibrations rise up a level. The secrets of the Prophets are revealed to the multitudes. The Goddess opens up the Tabernacle of Love to All. The unconscious is illuminated. Man and Woman Unite.

There are many signs of the Dawn. Always during major periods of Regeneration there is a pulsating and harmonic current of new Sound that is heard in the auric spaces. People begin to Dance. The Dancers come first. And then come the Midwives. Woman Spirit Rises and the Daughters of the Mother return to serve the Goddess. There is celebration on the Birthing Ground.

When the Dancers begin to Dance and the Midwives return it is a clear sign that it is Creation Time. The destiny of this earth is controlled by the Will of Creation. Not the scientists of destruction. This earth belongs to the Love-Spirit. God does not will that we blow ourselves up. God's will is Love. God's will is for all people on earth to realize they belong to the same Mother and Father. God's will is for Humanity to join together as One Unified Family. God's will is for a great and wonderous unification.

True power is Love. Those who have power have nothing to fear. Those in power do not project evil upon others. The men who rule the world do not have power. They have weapons of destruction and armies of confused young men. Their wars, at the expense of us all, are a mockery of God's will, a blasphemy of the Divine Word, and a slander of Truth.

During periods of Rebirth the axis of the earth shifts and the power centers of the planet alternate. A new Song can be heard. The bough of the Tree of Life bends to the East. The Table is set for a Sabbath Feast. The whole singing planet is ready for Love. Real revolution is about Love. Not oil, sugar, steel, or plutonium. Or that doctrine. Or that ideology. All the petty distinctions which used to divide us are washed away. No more big sounding words to justify war. No more alibis in the hypocritical store. No more genocide at our back door. No more pious justifications for the annihilation of nature.

This is Manifestation Time. Time for the Divine Revolution. Time to Live the Golden Rule. Life is to Be Lived, not codified into belief systems. Love never happens according to systems. Even the most evolved systems are restrictive of Love. Love and Truth are the Wings of the One-Heart. Love and Truth are always about Now. Change is the Way of Life. The earth constantly spins around the Sun. The ground is always fertile when the Seed of Truth grows.

Listen to the Midwives calling in the Dawn. Hear the Sacred Music and Sing the Sacred Song. Move from the Ground up and the Inside out. Make your culture good for the babes and the Grandmothers alike. This is the real revolution. Plant a seed that has never been sown and tend the fields of Creation. Bend down and sway in the Ancient Way. Listen to the call of the future. Let the New Life come forth. It is time to praise the Sun. Holy is the gypsy morning. Holy is the Light of Day. Holy is the Dancing Ground that makes the Whole World Sway. Holy is the Seed. Holy is the Golden Egg. Holy is the Unity of the Trinity and the Divinity of the One. All the Children of Earth are Holy.

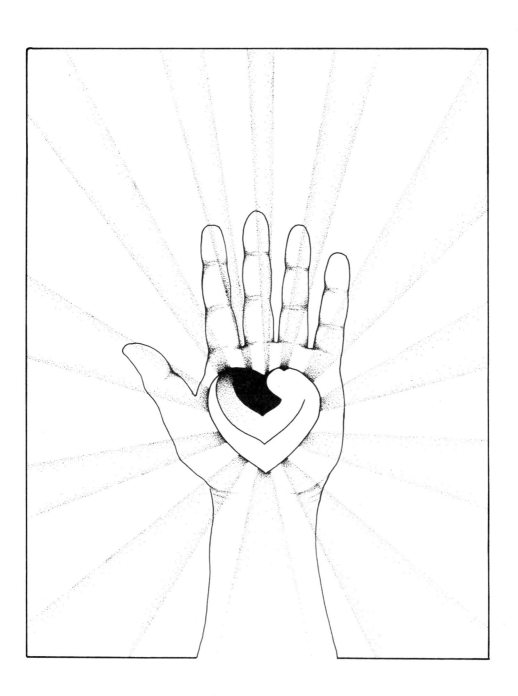

# BOOK ONE
# PROCREATION

All that we are can be traced back to the truthful whispers of a naked man and woman. We are all Children of Love. We belong to Love. We come from Love and return to earth to Love. This is the purpose of Incarnation.

# CHAPTER ONE

# RISING IN LOVE
## Conscious Conception

The purpose of family is to protect the Divinity in each of its members. The womb is always Eden. And now is always Holy. Wherever there is a man and woman, the ground is turned into a fertile garden. They open up the window of Heaven and call forth the Holy Spirit. They glorify the Presence. Indeed, wherever there is the Divinity of the fertilized egg there is the Holiness of Creation.

## Rising in Love

Each human is a vessel for Divinity. We are all made from Love. We are all Divine, from the root to the crown, from the top of what is up to the bottom of what is down. Love generates the nuclear family. The family is the basic unit of culture. Family can only be built by men and women working together. Culture is only as healthy as the cord that connects mother, father, and child.

A healthy culture teaches its Children how to walk the good road and rebel against that which is wrong and deathly. The family is charged with the task of keeping truth alive. No other social institution is as well equipped to protect and nurture. The family is the basic unit of protection for each egg that is hatched from the warmth of Love. It is the best way to care for the young.

## On the Rug

One way to foster conscious conception is to share spiritually-oriented time together each day. Conscious conception implies a deep capacity for parents to work out their differences within a spiritual framework. Indeed, it is not really possible to live with another unless there is a larger foundation for the relationship.

Daily clearing and conscious sharing allow the fulfillment of relationship. The time to do this must be seized from the pace of the world. Have a special time and place to do this work. A rug is a good space to work on, as it is a symbol for a place of prayer.

All over the earth, human beings weave rugs to tell their stories. Rugs are teachers — they transmit knowledge in their designs. A rug is a plane that softens the elements. Lovers on the rug gaze at each other's beauty. Within this context of mutual support,they take turns sharing what is current. This is a safe place to bring up things that may be hard to deal with. It is a safe place to bring up things that are purely gracious. After a while, lovers learn to appreciate this space, despite its intensity. They begin to realize that having this time saves them much energy spent gnawing on the bones of the past. Being on the rug together comes to be cherished as a necessary part of each day.

If this practice proves itself to be valuable, the lovers can actually design their own rug. They may even learn to weave or seek out a weaver in the neighborhood who can translate their idea on to fabric. Then they will have a rug from their hearts. It is much like a wedding ring. They may let it catch their tears. On it they honor the earth, soar in Heaven and participate in the miracle of life. They may wish to conceive their children on this special rug.

All Souls are One. We all come to earth to Love. Each time we take a Body we do so to realize Love. Love is the goal of the Soul. Love makes the two — One. When a man and woman link up their energies to bring forth new life all the best forces in the universe line up and serve them. Truly, the Goddess is pleased. She wants her daughters to be well cared for while they are filling with new life.

Before you conceive take time to dialogue with your partner. Dream and pray. Learn to channel your energy clearly. By doing this you serve all. When a man and woman rise in love they generate peace for all of humanity. And for themselves. Conscious union is the most vital step on life's journey. It's where we all come from.

Indeed there is no more pressing item on the consciousness raising agenda than family unity. Divorce is one of the most hurtful experiences of life. Nothing has so drained the creative energy of the American people. The custody battles (children are property in patriarchy) and fights over money between two people who once "loved" each other are the stark manifestation of the confusion that surrounds gender.

In Reality, all children are conceived consciously in the mind of God. The Divine One loves babies. The fact that the parents may not "want" a child does not in any way alter the Holiness of the babe. All Conception is Holy. Everyone is holy. Holy is the purpose of consciousness. Holy is the Body. Holy is the Spirit. Life on earth is sacred. All children are worthy. It is grace being on this sweet earth. To gaze upon the earth from any vantage point is a blessing. Every child is conceived under lucky stars. Upon conception there is no discrimination. Being inside the womb is one of the most blessed periods of every Incarnation. Such is the way of Creation.

When a man and woman can foresee their involvement, anticipate their duty, and take on cheerfully their Creation, the Goddess is happy. When two bodies merge in consciousness and the precise process of conception takes place with integrity, a peaceful ground is established for the newly incarnating Soul.

## O DIVINE ONE

Let the grace of your Love bond our hearts. Bless our intention to serve this child. Grant our resolve to build family. Help us grow together.

## O DIVINE ONE

As we join and bring forth new life, help us remember the origins of our love. As we conceive, may the Oneness of your Eternal Presence unify our love.

## O DIVINE ONE

Be our witness ~ In this act we both do solemnly promise to fulfill your Sacred Trust. ~

Sample Conscious Conception Contract: Sign on line and date

## A Conscious Conception

Perhaps the foremost researcher into conscious conception in the nation is Jeannine Parvarti Baker. She began fertility research while learning yoga and becoming fluent in the language of astrology. Her book *Hygieia*, published in 1978, is a compilation of her learnings in psychology and woman's health. She, without apology, addresses herself to those women who choose natural health and healing. Since that time she has maintained a consistent and fundamental investigation of issues which pertain to her sisters.

I asked Jeannine to share a story from her forthcoming book, *Conscious Conception: Elemental Journey Through the Labyrinth of Sexuality.*

## FERTILITY JOURNAL

Tracking our baby Quinn's first signal to us that he was ready to be conceived would have been difficult were it not for an unforgettable experience.

I HAD BEEN AWARE OF OUR NEXT BABY AROUND THE SKIRTS OF IMAGINATION, WAITING PATIENTLY FOR HIS PARENTS TO BEGIN THE CREATION DANCE.

However, we were struggling with this book and supporting our growing family and there seemed to be little support for another baby. Yet around the time that Quinn's call for incarnation came through, I suffered a serious accident. I sustained third, second and first degree burns in a sauna and convalesced for weeks doing lots of meditation.

I understood that knowing pain was integral to developing my healing powers for others. But the usual way medicine women acquire this knowledge by giving birth was not my experience. Giving birth has never been excruciating for me. I wouldn't voluntarily inflict suffering upon myself either by joining a heroic medicine society and being initiated into the mysteries of healing through pain. And so I have skimmed through life without any direct knowledge of outrageous pain. This thought helped some to cope with the searing pain which lasted weeks. But it was my relationship with Quinn as our pre-baby which was my greatest ally in foregoing pharmaceutical drugs or being admitted into a burn center/hospital for escape from pain.

During the height of my agony I heard Quinn's strong voice. "Stay alive, Mom! Don't give up! You can pull through the pain. I love you." When the burning hurt the most I could sometimes go out of my body (that is, disengage from feeling attached to the body) and it was in those altered states that Quinn came though loud and clear.

The thought of conceiving another baby with my husband was the most inspiring idea "to hang in there" as I lay in tremendous pain. I credit my quick recovery to the high spirits I maintained behind this fantasy of becoming pregnant once more.

After recovery was complete and I could walk again, Quinn became a constant companion. He told me many things through the feminine spirit voice. Already I had been dialoguing with this feminine voice and had named this spirit child "Hermione" after the Messenger-Goddess to the Greeks. Perhaps Quinn chose a male form in order to avoid that naming! In any case, when Rico and I began our preparations to conceive Quinn, it was under the guidance of Hermione, and no preference for either male or female baby.

With the romance of the universe in effect, we had our rendezvous during a tour I was making along the coast of California. Rico met me, fittingly enough, in a private sauna at a midwife-friend's home in Santa Cruz. We sparked in the way old lovers do so well. It had been a long separation for us — almost three weeks apart. There was change afoot in several ways, not the least being the offer to caretake the Terence McKenna's secluded Hawaiian home for the winter. My preference was to go home to Utah and conceive our baby. Yet we chose to begin our next pregnancy "in transit" — the favored way of Geminis.

The night of Quinn's conception was a soothing one. All seemed in order. Excitement generated by our decision to move to Hawaii (and miss one of the coldest winters on record in Utah) added to the anticipation of the unknown. Our ordinary miracle was about to begin.

## WE OPENED UP BODY-PRAYER TOGETHER

The mouths unfurl. All eyes turn together. Legs entwine the private parts. Skin grows slippery. Fingers in love mudras. Our breath slows, then rapids. River of ecstasy. Hopes spilling over. Filling and emptying again and again. Swirlingly still. We're riding the standing wave. And he is praying aloud with me.

"Dear Divine Parents, we are so grateful for Thy presence and infinite love. We thank Thee for this blessing of sexuality and the forms through which we worship Thee. Most kind Heavenly Father and Mother, we are humbled by Thy creation and are filled with awe at Thy power. We thank Thee for all our children, those here with us now, those who have already left the nest, and those yet to fly home to us. We thank Thee for our precious parents and all our ancestors who have given us this gift of life. And most happily we thank Thee for this lover, our mate, The One through whom we can touch Thee.

We ask Thee to guide and bless this conception so that it may be pleasing unto Thee. LET THY WILL BE DONE EMBODIED AS IT IS IN SPIRIT.

# Rising in Love

We ask Thee to bring great health, intelligence, strength, and wisdom so that this child can always be close to Thee and live Thy ways of peace with fullness of joy. Please grant this being the knowledge of its source. LET THIS BABY SERVE THEE IN ALL WAYS.

And lastly we hope that Thy blessing may extend to this couple so that these parents may open their hearts and be worthy co-creators with thee.

We say these things in the names of all Thy great teachers and Thy beloved son Jesus Christ who have come to Earth to show us who we really are.

Amen, and Blessed Be."

WE PRAY QUINN INTO EXISTENCE. MY SECRET PRAYER HOPING OUR BABY WILL ALWAYS KNOW THIS LOVE, FEEL THIS LOVE THAT BROUGHT HIM HERE IN THE FIRST PLACE.

A few days later our passion is heightened and the heat is on! The inner nest is building and fresh hope dwells in the soul. Along with teaching we also play — a night at the dance hall is up for us. Children settled in with friends we fly off to the civic auditorium for reggae dancing. A night at the concert opening our bodies up for sublime surrender. Let the music carry us blissward! During the ecstatic opening of the headliners, I HAVE A VISION AS I FEEL MY WOMB SURFACE THE SKIN OF MY SEX.

THE SPACE SHUTTLE ARRIVES ON THE MOON. THE EARTH RECEIVES THE WATERED SEED. THE CELL INLETS ANOTHER PROTEIN. A NEW IDEA IS ACCEPTED. THE SISTER JOINS THE SORORITY, HAZING COMPLETE. THE MOTHER OPENS HER ARMS UP TO HER CHILD, HUGGING CLOSEST. THE JELLYFISH EATS. THE NET CATCHES THE FLYING ARTIST. THE ORCHESTRA FINISHES TUNING UP. THE LOVERS REACH SECOND BASE. THE AFTERBIRTH IS EXPELLED. THE BALL MAKES IT THROUGH THE BASKET. THE YEAST FALLS INTO THE BREAD; I AM BAKERWOMAN GOD. THE ZYGOTE IMPLANTS IN THE UTERUS.

That night I dream of burying myself into warm sand. There is a cluster of sisters about me. They are chanting "into the ring of mugwort."

I am participating in some ritual, some woman's mystery and these sisters are helping me matriculate. The feeling is a sacred one and I feel personally very honored and accepted into the fold.

THE PELVIS KNOWS. THE DREAM CONFIRMS WHAT IS ALREADY FELT. I AM PREGNANT, IMPLANTED AND WILL WALK THE MOTHER'S PATH AGAIN.

■   ■   ■

Angel

**LOVE ALL THE CHILDREN AS ONE**

**THEY ARE ALL HOLY**

## Pre-Conception Diet

Conscious conception requires preparation on the physical as well as on the emotional and spiritual planes. Before conception, a purification process should begin in both parents. This involves the integration of healthful living habits and the elimination of harmful ones. All toxic substances and non-nutrifying foods should be eliminated. This includes such substances as coffee, sugar, alcohol, marijuana, tobacco, refined oils and starches, white sugar, and chemicalized water.

Fresh fruit and vegetable juices, salads, and raw nuts and seed combinations can be enjoyed. Yogurt and raw milk may be used. The main thing is to eat lightly and purely to allow the body to detoxify without becoming overly depleted and fatigued before conception.

Protein is needed to sustain the sexual and regenerative organs. Protein and sexuality are intricately linked. The daily flow of sexual energy has a crucial effect upon the distribution of hormones throughout the endocrine system. To have a healthy, fertile sexual life, one has to eat a good, rich diet. Whenever the diet does not include complex carbohydrates and complete proteins, there is a decrease in sexual vitality (perfect for periods of contemplation or celibacy but not for pre-conception). To maintain an active ejaculatory, ovulatory, and orgasmic sexual life, it is essential to find an optimal protein balance.

Timing is very important. Too much protein at any meal, especially at the end of the day, may actually be destructive to the body. And, if too many protein-rich foods are eaten at any one time, there can be an impairment of overall assimilation.

Optimal protein assimilation can only occur when the body is in a state of sugar balance. When blood sugar balance is maintained by such complex carbohydrates as whole grains, the protein we eat can be used for regenerative purposes; otherwise, it is used as fuel. Addicts of sugar and refined carbohydrates often confuse protein hunger signals with the need for a new sugar "hit".

Learning the amount and kind of protein to eat is essential for a high level of well-being. A vegetarian diet utilizing combinations of vegetables, grains, legumes, seeds, and nuts can supply excellent protein. However, vegetarians must be conscious of their protein intake. Too little protein interferes with our body's ability to maintain health and energy.

## Nutrition During Pregnancy

Pregnancy is a time to eat and gain weight without guilt. It is a time to focus on building the body. If the diet is natural and well-balanced and junk food is avoided, the weight gained will be perfectly healthy. Of course, what constitutes a "natural" diet for one mother may not be suitable for another. But there are basic guidelines which insure optimal fetal development and enable the mother to return to her pre-pregnant weight.

Environment must be taken into account to determine a diet that is adequate. The diet of an inner city mother must be substantially more protective than the diet of a mother who lives in a relatively tranquil environment. The following guidelines from the Society for the Protection of the Unborn Through Nutrition (SPUN), have been developed on the basis of years of clinical experience with thousands of pregnant women. The guidelines are presented in chapter five of *The Five Standards for Safe Childbearing* by David Stewart. I am grateful to him for permission to quote this section from his chapter entitled "Good Nutrition: The First and Fundamental Standard." My comments adapt the numbered information for those who have already begun to make substantial and healthful changes in their diets.

*". . . a pregnant mother should have every day, at least, the following or its equivalent (as recommended by . . . SPUN):*

*1. One quart of milk (whole, 2% skim, or buttermilk). Milk contains the second highest quality form of protein available, calcium, other minerals, and important vitamins. Natural (unprocessed) cheese and cottage cheese are about as good as milk.*

According to my nutrition teacher, Dr. Henry Bieler, raw milk is the only suitable milk for growing healthy bodies. His perceptions were based on the pioneering work of the Pottenger Foundation where generations of cats were fed both on raw and pasteurized milk. The findings were conclusive: raw milk was the nutrient that enabled the cats to reproduce normally and maintain health. Goat's milk is far superior to cow's milk.

For most people it is far better to eat two salads a day than to drink milk.

*2. Two eggs. Eggs have the highest quality source of protein, which is needed in large amounts to build your baby's brain. Eggs also have many more nutrients than any other food.*

Tibetan Buddhists regard the egg yolk as "golden medicine." Raw egg yolk (from the eggs of healthy, naturally-fed hens) is perhaps the most important food for rebuilding exhausted adrenal glands. Egg yolk is rich in iron, phospholecithins (which digest cholesterol), and vitamins E and A. There are many ways to creatively use raw egg yolk. One is to add it to a blender drink of raw milk, banana, and nutritional yeast, another is mix it in with cooked grain and vegetables in place of butter. It is best not to combine eggs with other concentrated proteins.

*3. Two servings of poultry, lean beef, fish, pork, lamb, or veal. If you are a vegetarian, alternatives to meat which are also rich in protein include: rice WITH beans, cheese, sesame, or milk; cornmeal WITH beans, cheese, tofu, or milk; beans WITH bulgar, cornmeal, wheat noodles, sesame seeds, or milk; peanuts WITH sunflower seeds or milk; whole wheat bread or whole wheat noodles WITH beans, cheese, peanut butter, tofu or milk. In vegetarian diets it is important to eat combinations of different kinds of protein foods together in order to receive the full nutritional benefits they contain.*

Choosing the source of one's protein is a highly personal affair and involves much thought as well as moral questioning. It is especially important that meat not be eaten out of habit or used as a stimulant. If meat eating has begun to make you feel sluggish, (a) eat less meat, (b) eat only rarely-cooked meat, (c) eat meat only with raw or steamed vegetables, (d) eat meat earlier than 6 p.m. and/or try substituting vegetarian alternatives.

The calcium/phosphorus ratio of seeds and nuts is especially beneficial. To be properly assimilated, they should be raw, fresh, unsalted, and then ground or soaked. Almonds, sesame, and sunflower seeds are very good during pregnancy. I believe that the peanut is not a suitable food. It is highly acidic and is often contaminated with toxic fumigants and anti-bacterial agents.

*4. Two servings of fresh greens, such as mustard greens, turnip greens, beet greens, spinach, collard greens, cabbage, kale, and parsley. These foods contain iron, other minerals and vitamin A and C. The darker the color, the better.*

Fresh vegetables provide us with the living enzymes and rejuvenating catalysts necessary to good health. They provide vitamin C in its most beneficial state. They are the most effective food for neutralizing acidic conditions. They are soothing foods for the system. An effective combination of vegetables is: steamed zucchini, string beans, celery, and parsley. This formula was derived by Dr. Bieler, and has proved itself again and again in therapeutic situations. It is rich in organic sodium (the main constituent of the liver) as well as organic potassium, which aids in the rebuilding of pancreatic enzymes.

Below is a brief sketch of some of our most common vegetables:

*Beets* — Build up red corpuscles in the blood and are an excellent bulk food high in vitamin C and potassium.

*Carrots* — their juice approximates the constituents of mother's milk. They increase resistance to colds and infection because of their supply of vitamins A and C. They also contain generous amounts of vitamins B, D, and E.

*Celery* — is a highly beneficial nerve food and an important source of organic sodium. It is rich in calcium and potassium also. The leaves of celery contain a substance akin to insulin.

*Chard* — rich in sodium and minerals.

*Lettuce* — is a calming food rich in folic acid.

*Onions, garlic* — are vastly useful for fighting infections. Garlic is an incredible herb used in treating arthritis, high blood pressure, and cancer. Both garlic and onions are rich in sulphur.

*Parsley* — noteworthy for fighting infection. It also helps maintain proper functioning of the thyroid gland and abounds in vitamin A.

*Potatoes (white, red, and yams)* — are excellent winter foods rich in digestible carbohydrates and minerals.

*Spinach* — a natural source of vital amino and nucleic acids, as well as iron and folic acid (essential in pregnancy).

*String Beans* — are notable for their potassium content and are a specific for all neutralizing diets and those aimed at restoration of the pancreas and liver.

*Winter Squash* — is a fine source of easily digestible carbohydrates blessed with vitamin A and rich in iron and magnesium.

*Zucchini* — a specific for the liver with its rich supply of organic sodium.

*Seaweed* — is also a vegetable. Whether eaten fresh, dried, or in powdered form, it is a valuable addition to the diet, containing all trace minerals in a balanced form — including organic iodine, which the thyroid gland needs to maintain metabolic homeostasis and promote healthy fetal development.

*5. Two of any of these: a whole potato, large green pepper, broccoli, grapefruit, orange, lemon, lime, papaya, or tomato. On occasion, unsweetened fruit or vegetable juice may be used as a substitute. These foods have a large amount of vitamin C, which helps protect you from infections and miscarriage.*

It is best to use supplemental vitamin C rather than out-of-season or chemically-produced fruits. If fresh, organically and locally grown fruits are available, they are beneficial and cleansing. Properly ripened, they contain essential vitamins and minerals. They should be eaten between meals, alone, or with dairy products. It is not good to eat fruit before a meal because they dilute and alkalinize digestive enzymes and secretions, making absorption of grain or protein foods more difficult. In general, fruits should not be eaten with vegetables although the apple is an exception to this. The apple is rich in potassium and magnesium and contains valuable digestive enzymes and a fair amount of vitamin C.

*6. Five servings of whole grain breads, cereals, or rolls. Brown rice, whole grain cornbread, and whole grain pancakes or waffles are equally good for you and your baby. Whole grains are foods that have not had their vitamins and minerals removed. They are usually rougher, darker, and heavier than enriched grains. Be sure you eat at least five servings of these foods every day, because they are rich in B vitamins and many minerals. (Enriched foods have very low amounts of these important vitamins and minerals and are NOT a substitute for whole grains).*

Whole grains maintain the proper blood sugar balance by being absorbed gradually into the bloodstream, thus protecting the vital force of the organism. Here follow capsule descriptions of the important grains:

*Brown Rice* — is rich in sodium, potassium, phosphorus.

*Millet* — is an alkaline grain and a very digestible protein, rich in nitrilosides.

*Oats* — are rich in calcium and silicon.

*Wheat* — is beneficial especially in its sprouted state, when its gluten, difficult for many to digest, has been transformed into an easily-digestible sugar.

*Corn* — is rich in lecithin and pro-vitamin A and E and is cooling to the system, thus a good warm weather grain.

*Buckwheat* — is rich in rutin, a component of vitamin C.

*Barley* — is a very soothing food for the inner linings of the intestines and is rich in B vitamins.

*7. Three tablespoons of butter or natural oil, such as corn, peanut or safflower oil. These provide important nutrients. Also, butter has vitamin A, and natural oils are rich in vitamin E. (Lard, bacon fat and other greases are not nearly as good).*

Olive oil and sesame oil are the only two oils that can be extracted without high heat. Heating oils breaks them down, making them more difficult to metabolize. As for butter, its use must be qualified, as chemical residues collect in milk fat.

*8. One serving of liver each week. Liver has much more iron and vitamin A than any other food and is a storehouse of protein, B vitamins, and other valuable nutrients. Vegetarians should eat a good quality brewer's yeast daily as an alternative to liver.*

I think this is very sound advice.

*9. One yellow or orange vegetable or fruit at least five times each week. These fresh fruits and vegetables have vitamins that protect you from infections.*

Again, I stress organically grown, locally produced fruits and vegetables.

*10. Salt — Salt your food to taste. Salt is an essential nutrient.*

Most Americans eat ten times too much salt. Use sea salt in small amounts.

*11. Water — Drink to thirst. (Note that water is specified here. Other beverages, even healthful, nutritious ones, are not a substitute for Water.)*

Learning one's water requirement is very important in establishing a sound nutritional life. Good clean water is an important, essential food. Restriction of water by those adhering to a strict macrobiotic diet has been linked to a high incidence of miscarriage. You will know you are drinking enough water if your urine is clear.

*12. Vitamin and mineral pills. These may be used as added insurance, they don't replace the values of good foods. It is completely safe to take most vitamins and minerals, but certain ones, such as iron, can be harmful in large doses.*

Of course, the best way to get one's vitamins is through our food, but unless our food is carefully and organically grown, it is sadly deficient. Food that is mass-produced on depleted soils and contaminated with pesticides cannot be optimally nourishing. But if you are eating well, and still feel a lack of energy, you may need to supplement your diet with vitamins.

Heavy vitamin supplementation is not appropriate for everyone. In a naturopathic sense, the cause of physiological impairment is seen as a depletion of vital force, so it is by no means certain that energy imbalance can be laid at the doorstep of vitamin deficiency. But in most cases there are sufficient nutritional side effects from imbalance to make vitamin therapy very rewarding. The following, then, are brief descriptions of some of the vitamins that may aid us in our nutritional transformation:

*Vitamin A* — is best obtained from both animal and vegetable sources, since an impaired liver cannot synthesize carotene. Use a vitamin A preparation made from fish liver oils, lemon grass and other herbs. It is important that this vitamin is fresh. Oils do go rancid. Vitamin A supplements should be taken with foods rich in this vitamin, such as egg yolk, liver, winter squash, carrots, sweet potatoes, turnip greens, parsley, persimmons, apricots, lemon grass, and dandelion greens.

A basic recommended daily dosage would be 25,000 units, after meals containing oils. There has been a great scare about vitamin A toxicity. This can happen, to be sure, through reckless pill-popping or chomping polar bear liver, but it is a highly improbable danger.

*Vitamin B Complex* — are significant stress vitamins especially fortifying for contemporary nervous systems which must receive, compute, and program an incredible amount of input from the "power-grid world." As the world's increasing demands impinge upon our skins and nerves, the need for this vitamin complex increases exponentially.

The B vitamins are water-soluble so can penetrate into every cell of the body. They flow with water, they are light, and they have to do with responses that move like light within the entire nervous system. They are a supreme nerve food.

The need for vitamin $B_6$, pyridoxin, increases immediately after conception. When it is undersupplied, an amino acid from protein cannot be utilized normally; instead it is converted into a substance known as xanthuretic acid, which is excreted in the urine. The more of this acid excreted, the more severe is the vitamin $B_6$ deficiency. Urine tests have shown that 95% of all pregnant women are deficient in $B_6$. Magnesium and $B_6$ work in interrelated ways. Magnesium is necessary before enzymes containing $B_6$ can help build red blood cells. Magnesium deficiencies are common in America. $B_6$ works through our adrenal glands to stimulate secretions.

It is difficult to discuss the role of vitamins without relating them to the networks of relationships that they influence. For example, sulphur, essential to body tissues and proper digestion, is also needed for the synthesis of vitamin $B_1$. $B_1$, like niacin, is a specific for depression and anxiety. $B_{15}$ and folic acid help oxygenate red blood cells. Folic acid is crucial during pregnancy. It is essential for the formation of both DNA and RNA. One fifth of all pregnant women are deficient in folic acid. A $B_{12}$ deficiency is often found in people who, voluntarily or involuntarily, live on a diet of fruit and vegetables with no animal foods. $B_{12}$ is found in foods of animal origin, including small amounts in honey.

The balance between the various B vitamins is also important. Morning sickness in pregnancy is almost always a sign of B vitamin deficiency or imbalance. Our B-vitamin balance also crucially affects the thyroid — which in turn is affected by blood sugar levels. When our liver is impaired, our entire B-vitamin balance becomes skewed so that we need to make corrections with sensitive use of B-vitamin-rich foods, such as: nutritional yeast, whole grains, yoghurt, seeds and nuts, liver, miso, and eggs. B-vitamin supplements should be taken with meals containing foods high in the B Complex vitamins. It is important that the B vitamins in supplemental form be in a balanced formula. All B vitamins must be supported with minerals such as molybdenum, copper, and magnesium (vital to the transport and synthesis of hemoglobin).

*Vitamin C* — is found in living foods, fresh foods. It is the "freshness factor" and it keeps us fresh by bringing oxygen to our cells. Vitamin C transports iron in red blood cells, thus increasing our absorption of iron. Thus, through taking in good amounts of vitamin C, iron-anemia can be corrected without adding any iron to the diet. Vitamin C also aids the absorption of folic acid, pantothenic acid, and vitamin B2.

Vitamin C aids in fighting infections and facilitates detoxification. For city dwellers, it is wise to use anywhere from two to eight grams daily, dosage depending upon the extent and intensity of stress. If exposed to exhaust fumes, tobacco smoke, fluorescent light, air conditioning and gas heat, or with psychological pressure, eight grams is not too much.

Vitamin C, like the B vitamins, is water soluble and so can penetrate into every cell of our body. However, it is not stored in the body; excess is eliminated and there is no danger of overdosing. I have heard people say that, since excess is excreted from the body, it is a waste of money to take large doses of vitamin C. However, before it is processed and the excess eliminated, the vitamins do course through the body and have a chance to catalyze our defense system in a positive way.

*Vitamin D* — the sunshine vitamin. The sun's rays meet the living skin and a process is initiated that metabolizes this vitamin. The best time for hunting and gathering this vitamin is mornings, when the sun's ultra-violet light is the most absorbable. An adequate supply of vitamin D is important since, for one thing, it promotes the proper absorption of calcium and phosphorus. Fine food sources of vitamin D are egg yolks, fish liver oils, sunflower seeds, shitake mushrooms, nettles, and milk (especially in summer). Be careful with supplemental vitamin D. It is stored in the body, in the liver, bone, skin, and brain. You *can* over-dose with it. 600-800 International Units are recommended during pregnancy.

Pregnancy is a perfect time to establish good nutritional patterns. The physical body is a cybernetic system. A good nutritional pattern liberates one's attention from the gross level of desire, and fulfills a primary need of the entire organism. A good nutritional pattern integrates body and mind so that the Spirit can soar free.

## Serving Her

There are many ways to serve the pregnant woman. Bring tea and comfort, a listening ear. Bring a message of hope and courage. Bring a willingness to hear truth. During the pregnant moons the truth will grow within her body. She becomes sensitive to the Core of reality, to the One-Heart. She is in an exalted biological state.

Neil Amber

Mother, teach us. Sometimes we forget how best to be at your service. Remind us. Speak up. Let your needs be known. These times are yours. There is nothing we would rather do than serve you.

Heed the Call, Children. She is ready
to fly day and night. She has no fright.
She is a light beam. She is courage in
motion. She is sweet with devotion.
Her helpers are among the first to arrive
and the last to leave. She does what is
right because she knows what is right.
She has learned well from her sisters.
She knows how to breathe in the purity
of Life. Grandmother is very proud of
Her.

# CHAPTER TWO

# LISTENING TO THE MIDWIVES
## Setting the Priorities

The first thing to do after discovering you are pregnant is to give thanks to the Goddess, and then to stock up on the finest, freshest organic foods available and cease any activities that may interfere with your child's development. The next step is to find a midwife. It is now possible for every mother to have a friend beside her while giving birth. It is now possible for every mother to have an ally to help her as her family is regenerated.

I have seen my midwifery teacher walk into the birthroom and give the laboring mother an attention so total that it allowed her to relax, experience her own power, and let her baby out. It is now possible for every birthing mother to have a friend to help her feel the Holiness of birth.

## Listening to the Midwives

Oh how I wish my mother could have been blessed with the service of a midwife — of a helper who knew what it was like to be born again while giving birth. All women deserve to have a friend by their side. All mothers deserve support when they bond. Mothering must be protected from the evils of patriarchy and protected by the Laws of the Land.

Midwives have existed in all times to usher in new life. The midwives who picked Moses from the reeds and those who serve the Goddess in the Inner City today are the Same Being. In a vital culture there are always those whose primary work is to serve pregnant women. The women who serve women always exist. Midwifery is a healing art which stands outside the dominion of the medical-industrial-complex.

All Mothers need the support of wise women to guide them into their new role as nurturer of the young. They need the guidance of women who clearly perceive the spiritual dimensions of motherhood as well as the economic, marital and societal concerns. Every mother is involved in a deeply spiritual process when she opens up to give birth and this process must be honored, respected, and protected by her community, network and clan.

I rest easier at night knowing there are now many women whose sole work is to teach their sisters the truth about birth and bonding. There is a steadily growing international network of midwives who serve Life. All across our nation, the practice of midwifery is thriving. It is in the forefront of new age occupations. No computer programmer is ever going to put midwives out of business. Midwives are the wise women of the Divine Revolution.

Whenever I get discouraged about the violent ways of the world or the election of some president, I remember these women. Whenever my attention is called to the prison cell of a political prisoner, I remember the new ones being born. Their numbers are growing. Someday, very soon, the Freedom Loving people of America are going to stand up and demand that the harassment of midwives be stopped. Soon, very soon, the day will come when it will be against the law to interfere with birthing ways. As more and more babies are born at home the tyranny of centralized medicine will be abolished.

Soon, very soon, there will be millions and millions of us who are ready to acknowledge our common roots in the Soul of Love. The day is fast approaching when all of humanity will realize they originate within the Rainbow Mother. By celebrating the return of new life and the ways of the Goddess we help usher in the Light of

Truth. By praising the Holiness of the womb we establish ourselves upon the fundamental ground of Being. By giving mid-wives a central role in the decision-making processes of culture we begin the long process of revitalizing the primary matrix of life.

The following midwives represent some of the major constituen-cies of the American population. They work in the Inner-City and in the Eastern plains of Oregon. They work in border towns helping the brown-skinned poor and in Beverly Hills. Midwifery is flourishing and the ways of birthing are once again revolving around the needs of the people.

## A MIDWIFE SPEAKS FROM THE INNER CITY

*Dear Joshua,*

*Some of us have chosen to work with women in hospitals. The work there is certainly no less holy, for all births evoke the face of the God-dess. The women who birth in hospitals — through fate, through choice, through true medical need — also have the right to traditional midwifery and its loving, personalized and empowering care.*

*The tradition of midwifery is not something defined by age or gender or social position. Men can be midwives. Childless women can be mid-wives. Doctors can be midwives. This tradition is not defined by the absence of technology. If midwifery as a service is as ancient as heal-ing, it must also keep pace with Twentieth Century knowledge — it must accompany women who go to the hospital, who need drugs to start their labors, whose bodies are invaded by electronic monitoring.*

*True midwifery is not defined by the site of the birth or the gender of the provider. It is defined by the quality of caring, the level of empathy, the faith in the birth process, the commitment to wholism, to ex-cellence, to skill and to INDIVIDUALIZATION. True midwifery is an act of love — whether we are reimbursed for it directly or whether our com-munity supports us as we provide it free of charge.*

*This tradition of care must never become the exclusive prerogative of the rich or the privileged. Poor women deserve this care as much as rich women do; Third World women need it as much as white women do. Most American women now give birth in the hospital, and to abandon the hospital is to abandon the majority of American women. Most women of color have been persuaded that a hospital birth is better and safer than birthing at home, and that it represents the first class care that racism and sexism have denied their mothers. There is a strong tradition of Southern Black midwives because racist-run Southern hospitals refused to admit Black women. There is a strong desire for hospital birth among Laotian women who have watched helplessly as their babies died in refugee camps and who want the "best American" care for their newest child.*

# Listening to the Midwives

*As an inner city midwife, I work with "the people" — with poor women, with Third World women, with teen-aged women, with single women. A wholistic practice here means attention to norms that are not middle class as well as scrupulous commitment to those norms which are part of human and humane birth practices worldwide. For example, all of our patients want their right to privacy respected. All of them want to be accompanied by the support person or persons of their choice.*

*However, that support person may not be the husband: a family-centered birth for a Laotian or Cambodian family may be one in which the husband waits outside the birthing room, or is not even physically present in the hospital; because in that culture, men do not directly participate in birth. A wholistic practice in my setting means fighting the hospital administration who wants to make "early discharge" a prerequisite for use of the Alternative Birth Center. Many of the multiparous women using our ABC want three day hospital stays with daytime rooming-in only. This hospital time may be a woman's only respite from total household responsibility; a time of pampering, away from sexist or unsupportive husbands, the numerous and competing demands of other children, and the continual demands of household chores. A time when someone else cooks her meals, feeds and changes her baby at night, and cleans her environment may represent a true vacation for the woman — even if it takes place in a hospital and only lasts two days.*

*We have finally begun to understand that childbirth is at least a physiologic, a psychologic, a spiritual, and a culturally mediated event. For those of us who work with the poor, the delivery of midwifery care involves all of the preceding and is also a political and economic struggle. It is a struggle with our employers, doctors, hospital administrators and county health departments alike who look first not at the content of care but at its cost. Labor sitting, for example, which is such an integral part of private midwifery practice, has almost never been defined as NECESSARY to public and inner city practice and is never considered a reimbursable cost. It is not a part of many of our sister services, and we have had to struggle long, hard and creatively in order to insure that it continues to be part of the services we provide.*

*I've had to become aware of local legislators, and legislative practice, for the initial funding for our service and subsequent funding for some of our clinic has come out of special legislative efforts. One cannot serve the poor successfully and be estranged from the local political process.*

*In summary, I consider my midwifery practice, like my life, to be a dance on the edges of blades of grass. Do you know what it would take to dance on the edges of blades of grass? The delicacy, the struggle, the balance, the stress? It is a practice different from others, and yet, in core, the same. I've long believed that for those of us who serve the Goddess, she will be there no matter where we go. Whether we dance in the moonlight or take spaceships to the stars, she will be with us, for we carry Her in our hearts.*

*I Peace Keep on my staff, and lobby with local legislatures, and administer my service, but I still see God/dess in the face of every woman who gives birth. Whatever dance I do, this is the core of my service — and the commitment of my faith.*

■    ■    ■

# A MIDWIFE SPEAKS FROM A RURAL COMMUNITY

*From the Community:*

Ina May Gaskin is the leading midwife on "The Farm" in Tennessee. She is the author of *"Spiritual Midwifery",* and a strong voice for the re-emergence of the midwife.

Midwifery belongs to the people. It is a fundamental human right for a woman to choose the manner in which she will give birth. Native people of the world understand this, maintaining women in charge of women's reproductive affairs. No reasonable form of government can have authority over our most private affairs — how we are born and how we die. . .

Like the civil rights movement, the anti-war movement, and the anti-nuclear movement, the midwifery movement is a *consciousness-raising* effort. People need to be reminded that an alternative exists. We need to talk openly in our communities about childbirth; write letters to the administration of the local hospital; write letters to the newspapers. We must be vocal about what we think is right. People can let the doctors in their area know what they want in obstetrical care. A good way to do this is through meetings of people with similar feelings — those who recognize that birth is a sacrament that belongs to the family. People who are interested in helping should collect together and talk and discuss all the issues and study their facts and their history, and then seek out a doctor who thinks that what they want is something reasonable, and who would be willing to provide some apprenticeship-type training. Families who have already had their babies in some way that was satisfactory to them should be trying to collectively support a midwife, or someone who aspires to learn — somebody who's working positively toward providing alternatives. It can be a collective venture rather than having to support itself by charging fees for midwifery. That way it is not in such direct competition with the doctors . . .

Midwives need to improve their communications skills in order to communicate well with doctors. This is part of the art of midwifery. An angry attitude on the part of the midwife is not going to be helpful. A midwife can't harrass a doctor into helping her; it must be a friendly relationship. After all, she'll probably be calling him in the middle of the night . . .

If a midwife's motives are not selfish and she is practicing out of love, this will show. Any doctor who is going to commit himself to helping a midwife needs to know to what lengths she is willing to go to be careful and safe, and that she is not looking to expand her own fortunes but is genuinely dedicated to helping mothers and families who want something other than what they are able to get in the standard hospital situation . . .

Not every mother who would like a natural birth will actually be able to have one, so part of the midwife's job is to prepare couples who need to go to the hospital. When they arrive at the hospital, she can often do the talking and make the necessary arrangements to pave the way for the couple to have a satisfactory hospital experience. A midwife should have someone on her backup team who can perform cesareans . . .

A midwife in today's world has to have an expanded vision of her responsibilities. We've found that we can affect the whole way of life in our community.

A midwife should have a good relationship with her own husband so that she can counsel other couples effectively. In seeing a lot of couples through pregnancy and childbirth, through heavy trips when their children are being raised, you get an insight into how men and women relate to each other, and you can really be significant in helping people out.

Another major area where midwives work is teaching ladies how to breastfeed. Not only does the midwife draw on her own experiences, but if she's in any kind of community situation, she can make use of wet nurses and other babies that already know how to suck, to get a mother successfully breastfeeding. An important area is well-baby care, looking at babies that aren't sick. If there's anyone in your area that you're responsible for, check them out. A midwife should extend her protection to all the kids in her area as much as she can and really try to make that something real.

Nutrition counseling is an important function for a midwife, and well worth serious study. Don't just be concerned about what is being put into the baby's system during the prenatal period or what he's going to be fed after he's born. You need to learn about what's in the water, what the farmers are feeding their cattle, and what's being sprayed on the trees next door. It's up to the midwives and the doctors to know about these things.

Sex education of teenagers is an important area, particularly teenage girls who come into childbearing age before they're really ready to become parents. We need to protect these kids. The government hasn't given funding or encouragement for safe, effective, natural means of birth control. Sometimes a young girl will think she has to lay her boyfriend in order to keep him. She needs her consciousness raised. Sometimes you can let her know that if her boyfriend would leave her if she didn't lay him maybe she should have a better boyfriend. The midwife may be the only person who can tell her this.

## Listening to the Midwives

Parents also need to be counselled many times in child raising. It's a 24-hour job and it has its highs and its lows. If somebody's really strung out and tired, they need your continued help.

We think that midwives also have an important role in preventing wife and child abuse in their community. It is your business. The midwife's job is to see that it's okay for the ladies and the babies, and the men too. If there's somebody in your neighborhood that needs help, be brave enough to be the one to talk to them, and if you need to have your husband's help in that, enlist him to the cause, too. This is the only way that we're going to effectively be able to prevent that kind of trouble.

To maintain her level of competence at a reasonable level, the midwife is responsible for her own continuing education. She should be a never-ending student of the body and its processes. Friendly doctors, books, periodicals and other midwives are all good sources of information.

■　　■　　■

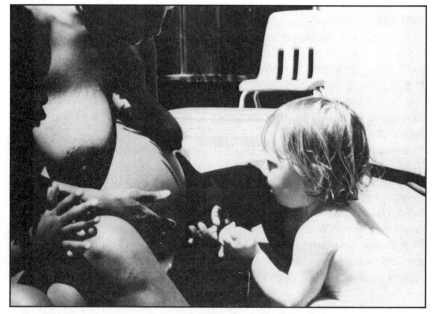

Ruth Katz

# A MIDWIFE SPEAKS FROM
# MIDWIVES ALLIANCE OF NORTH AMERICA

Elizabeth Davis is the author of a lucid book entitled *"A Guide to Midwifery: Heart and Hands"*. I spoke with her in her home in the summer of 1983. She had spent the morning teaching and her students were still there when I arrived. I could feel the deep trust among them all. After they left we went into the kitchen. She made some tea and we began to chat. While she spoke, I felt the kindling of ancient roots — the source of this woman's nurturance.

**Elizabeth:** My work with MANA (Midwives Alliance of North America — see end of interview for further information) is an attempt to organize midwives toward greater visibility. This is the only way we are going to survive. There are some midwives who are anti-organization, who fear that any effort to regulate or define midwifery will squelch it and take the artistic creation away. They think that as soon as you make standards, you get caught in standardized practice — and midwifery is not a standardized practice. However, it all depends on the kinds of standards and how sweeping they are. All MANA is trying to do now is find a basic framework, a basic agreement on our role. We don't have to nit-pick particulars. We are not setting up a licensing apparatus. We can be self-regulating.

An alliance can give us a sense of identity through networking, and also a vehicle for evolving our current art form. It keeps our work out of the hands of the state — at least, temporarily. We must define midwifery so we can shape it to suit the needs of today. This is a step we have to make. If we don't do this, midwifery may be eliminated. Do you know how many arrests occurred in the last six months? Five or six. No incidents at delivery. They just knock on the door, come in, search your house.

**Joshua:** What's to be done?

**Elizabeth:** Education. And what we are finding is that we don't have an educational model for midwifery. There are few institutions educating their students wholistically. It's certainly not being done in med. school. There it's the same old thing: running residents ragged. They're put on 24-hour call, four days a week — pushed and pushed, eventually so dehumanized that they buckle under. That's no way to train a midwife. A midwife is an independent practitioner. She must make her own decisions. She has to be resourceful.

So MANA is most helpful. This midwive's alliance is an association of lay and nurse midwives. The reason nurse midwives have joined is that many who have gone the nursing route have found an inevitable conflict between their real work and the identity they have within the medical profession. And whenever they speak to that conflict, they are being squelched. I think what we are finding is that we are all fundamentally midwives. The scope of our work is not encompassed by the medical profession as we know it. Midwifery is one of those New Age professions that hasn't really defined itself yet. It's developing. Even though it's as old as time, it's ancient primarily in a healing aspect. But as a modern-day profession, it's transitional. This is why midwives have to get together. It is very good that we are organizing on a larger basis. If MANA can network information all over the country and Canada and inspire midwives to organize regionally, perhaps MANA will eventually be able to offer its own certification and equivalency. Then we can establish a power base in the midwives' community itself.

My position in MANA is an interim one. It came to me at a time when my identity was wavering and I was feeling that lay-midwivery didn't really amount to much— maybe I'd just throw in the towel and go to nursing school after all. I've got children of my own and I didn't want to get arrested. (When was I going to give up this idealistic nonsense?) And then I got this appointment and I thought, how can I turn my back on my roots as a lay-midwife and drop everything and haul off and put my head under a microscope? There's a lot of important work to be done for the sake of the birthing couple. They deserve to have choices, to be treated like individuals and to be fostered not just through pregnancy, but throughout the process of becoming parents. They need someone to be there for them in this life transition in a very *real* way. With that ideal in mind, I got back some perspective.


**Joshua:** Hallelujah.


**Elizabeth:** Well, I'm one of the few lay-midwives left in San Francisco and it's gotten to the point where, if I were a pregnant lady, I don't know if I would be able to find the midwife I could trust to be at my birthing.

I understand the kind of strictures that nurse-midwives have to operate under. There's a midwifery service in Marin County that had a 50 percent transport rate for first-time mothers. They were forced to practice this way by the stringent standards of their medical back-up (no doubt determined in part by malpractice insurance). Now they have given up their home birth practice entirely.

This raises the question: how can one comfortably give birth if the midwife is psychologically divided? If she is not able to be honest and real with you because it's not a matter of assessing your situation for what it is, but of following doctors' rules, you no longer have a relationship based on trust. Parents are thus forced to abdicate responsibility; they no longer have the support or free decision-making.

I do not want to see midwifery lost. I think that midwifery is one of the cornerstones of the New Age. If people are empowered in birthing, then they translate that immediately into their experience of parenting. I consider my work successful if a woman says "I did it", not "You were so wonderful", or "I couldn't have done it without you". It's marvelous to see a father assist in the delivery of his baby or to watch parents lift their child up together in their own hands in that moment of utter release and revelation! That's what this is all about. There is (or should be) a transmutation of identity at this point, which the midwife supports by channeling energies. That is the real essence of her work.

People started having home births because they wanted to take responsibility. Things used to be a lot more black and white in the late 60's and early 70's: either you wanted to take responsibility and have a home birth because you were doing everything else on your own anyway (say homesteading with a cottage industry) *or* you simply did what was socially acceptable and had your baby in the hospital. Nowadays home birth has a certain novelty to it — it has become a fad. People sometimes come to me thinking in a conservative way about something that is basically unconventional. They believe they can pay me a certain amount of money and I'll take care of everything — I'll do their birth for them. All they have to do is to be nice to me, friendly and sociable and enjoyable and everything will go fine. They are invariably the couples that, around the 7th or 8th month (usually not before then — it's not before the birth becomes imminent that the edginess surrounding the reality surfaces), I need a 'get down' session with. I confront them with the games I see and the possible consequences of these during the birth. I simply state my unwillingness to take responsibility in areas where they're lacking.

And this is where the real learning begins to take place. This is where you see people clean up behavior patterns that have been with them for years. They begin to re-think ideas of what a mother is, what a father is. They begin to see that giving birth is not just for the baby. They have an opportunity, a chance at being reborn themselves. That's what the work is really about."

■   ■   ■

Indeed, that is what the work is all about. Thankfully, there are such women who are facilitating the continuity of that work. They need our support. They need our help, now.

Women who personally transmit an ancient human lineage must not only be capable of responding with intuition, knowledge, power and grace, but they must also withstand the attacks of a society that is heartbroken and bent on destruction. The current wave of repression against midwives is one of the most tragic expressions of the deep sickness of our society. The persecution of midwives will not end. But the persecution cannot succeed. It will fail because there are women who know that the truth of birth reveals the sacredness of humanity. And honoring this sacredness empowers us.

Midwives Alliance of North America (M.A.N.A.)
30 South Main
Concord, NH 03301

Brian Cook

Let us be clear that when I say Goddess, I am not talking about a being somewhere outside of this world. Nor am I proposing a new belief system. I am talking about choosing an attitude: choosing to take this living world, the people and the creatures on it as the ultimate meaning and purpose of life, to see the world, the earth, our lives as sacred.

Star Hawk

Children hear music while in the womb. We come to listen to the sound of our mothers' Heart. We are drawn to the Earth by the pulsations of the Cord of Creation. We belong to a Great Circle of Life. It is safe now on the Birthing Ground. The drums of Life are wailing.

# CHAPTER THREE

## BLESSING WAY
### In the Beginning Was Love

Now that the pregnancy is well underway and the new life is secure in the womb and the good hormones are flowing and She is generating the warmth and glow that only a pregnant woman can radiate, it is time to gather the community together to praise the Couple. Held on the waxing moon before delivery, The Blessing Way is a ceremonial gathering of friends and loved ones to honor the expectant couple. At a Blessing Way friends gather for one sole reason; To bless. To bless requires letting go of all bindings and it is a blessing to be invited.

The Blessing Way is a statement proclaiming the Holiness of Birth. By gathering the community together the isolation of pregnancy is transformed into a joyous sharing. The Blessing Way is not an astral plane ceremony. It is for the benefit of the earth. Now. The community showers the pregnant couple with gifts. In our community the women give very creative presents. One does not have to have money to help the birthing women. Childcare, meals, laundry, housecleaning, and shopping are all immensely appreciated.

The Blessing Way has an impact upon the pregnant couple as well as the community. I have found that I feel connected to the child in ways that are special. I remember well the first Blessing Way I attended. It was for Akasha. It was held by a stream in summer. The water formed a perfect birth canal and emptied into a big pool. I started floating down the stream on my back pretending I was being born. Akasha came in the water and started playing too. It was so beautiful to see her big belly floating down Mother Earth's birth canal. A few days later Akasha gave birth to a beautiful girl named Brooks. Brooks is a special friend to this day. The ground for our relationship was begun before she ever came out of the Womb, on the day of her Blessing Way.

If I am asked to organize a Blessing Way I like to have the men and women meet separately and then join together. This format allows a deeper level of sharing and opening. It is most instructive to younger men to meet in a circle with the expectant father. Such a circle strengthens the bonds between fathers and sons. When the men and women meet it is very powerful. True nuclear energy is generated.

I asked a few friends of mine to share stories of their Blessing Ways:

## MY BLESSING WAY

I had only just heard of the Blessing Way when I decided to give one in honor of our unborn child, now known as Zuri. As far as I know, ours was the first of many in our area. What was the Blessing Way to be? A ritual? a family gathering? a community event? . . . we had no boundaries. When planning our Blessing way, Sleeping Beauty kept coming to mind. The wisest women in our area must be asked to come and bless our child. And so it was that five of my closest and wisest womanfriends were asked to gather ahead of time and prepare whatever blessing they felt moved to create.

## Blessing Way

The day came, blue sky reflected in the mass of puddles, a gentle wind and crisp air . . . a fine day to raise the energy. It seems that, in relationships, when one is nervous the other is calm. So Chuck, Zuri's father, went to prepare the barn, the concrete world of getting the fire started, and to think on his own. For myself, I began to gather, finally, my thoughts on the material end of our ritual. I did not know, even then, what I would say, as is the case in most rituals, but I knew what was to be conveyed, and I prayed that I might be a clear channel to do just that. When Chuck came back we discussed what we both would like to do and that was that. We gathered our symbols of holiness and walked down to the barn.

The Blessing began with our friend John singing "Little Seahorse" by Bruce Coburn. With that the tides turned and I lost my nerve while Chuck regained his. Thank goodness we were sitting together and everyone else was smiling!

Grandpa Robert Hugs, the elder in our community, "smudged" each person in the circle with sage and cedar. This is a North American Indian custom for clearing energy in a sacred manner. Smudging everyone is also a way to focus attention, to bring people together as "one". I would like to add that Grandpa is ninety years old and looks like Santa and when this man smokes you, you feel as though all pettiness has been lifted from your shoulders.

I asked for a silent meditation. As we all held hands, I said, "We ask everyone here to focus on our child and with that thought bring in the happiest love-filled energy that you can and send it to the center of our circle. Then let that energy become a fountain that pours over all of us. Let us all bask in that moment."

Silence.

The silence was answered with the chant "ya-na-ho-we-ah-heyenae". Everyone joined in. I had sung this all through my pregnancy. It means "Great Spirit, make me as strong as a bear". It is a traditional North American Indian chant for women in childbirth. To bear the pain, the pain of surrender, the surrender to the most vulnerable place a woman knows and to wait only in expectation of the unknown — this is the lot that we've been asked to do as women. It is an honor.

During the chant, Chuck and I made our altar. The altar cloth was, ironically, a quilt I was making for Zuri, still with pins and needles in the border. On it we placed our directional feathers, pointing in the four directions, plus two more for the Earth Mother and the Heavenly Father. Then in each section we placed a "holy object". With the completion of our altar we all stopped singing.

Chuck recited from Gibran's *"The Prophet":* "Your children are not your children. They are the sons and daughters of Life's longing for itself . . ." and so on, through the entire stanza.

I then began prayers to the directions, asking the spirits that harbor there to grant to my child the attributes of that direction. With each direction Chuck handed someone sitting in that area of the circle a lighted candle. When my prayer was done, the candle was blown out to release my prayer unto the Universe. This was done in all the directions.

It was then that my wise women came in. They came in from the corners of the four directions, each bearing a promise to the child to-come. My midwife, Dora, talked of the changes Chuck and I would go through and asked that everyone there be witness to these changes and support us through the times ahead. (By the way, at this time neither of us was nervous. Spirit has the power to bring out the best in all of us.)

With my mother by my side we represented the generations. From one daughter to the next we pass down creation. The process of a billion years, the making of a race, a species, the human form. At the Blessing Way, we honor our mothers. It is rare that we understand that significance, that she gave birth to us; she faced the unknown to bring forth a child. My mother brought forth me. She brushed my hair at my Blessing Way to soothe me and, at the same time, to change the way I wear my hair. I wear my hair down (I did anyway) and so my Mother brought it back and tied it up. The point was for me to focus on my birth. For someone who wears their hair tied up, the hair would be let down so the energy would flow, and the mother be relaxed and surrender to the birth. If the hair is usually flowing down, the woman's mother will tie it up as a symbol of focusing energy. Again, the tradition is an honoring of our mothers, who can facilitate change in us so simply.

Next was another Navajo tradition: the herbal footbath. It is generally only for the midwife and mother, but in our ritual Chuck had his feet washed too. Here the midwife humbles herself. She is of service to the mother. She gently touches us with herbs and warm water. Her touch asks that I surrender to her, trust her . . . and her voice says, "Thank you for honoring me with the gift of your birth". Dora dried our feet with blue corn meal — the sacred powder of the plains Indians. Here we are treated in a Holy Way. It is now known that we have been prepared in a Holy Way to walk the new path set before us.

Love, Meryl
Meryl is a midwife and herbalist

This is what a male friend of mine said at his Blessing Way. There were about seven of his friends and the impact of his words were the same on all of us. And we all have come forward to be with his child, just as he asked.

## Blessing Way

"My brothers, it is so good that you are all here with me today as I enter this next stage of life. I need you here with me today. I need you to help me in this. There will be times that I will need you to be with my child when I need space. I want my child to have deep relationships with my men friends.

You know I waited a long time to become a father. I have worked hard to get myself together, to work out some stuff and you know I am still not ready in some ways. But my heart is ready. And I have been blessed to be with a woman whom I really think I can work together with.

As I look around this circle I know I am ready. To bring a child into such a circle of brothers is a blessing. I love you all.

■　　■　　■

*When the Sun stood at Midday, the Divine Husbandman caused the people of earth to come together. The Soul is once again Free to Return to the Goddess. Open my mouth. I'll pray you. From nothing. I am pregnant with you. Holy wind whistle through me. Been a long time since you had a pipe for this music.*

Jim Dionne

birth shield painted while pregnant during vision quest

davidburns

# ONE-HEARTED VISION

Rainbow Mother, Nurturing Mother
Mother of us All
Suckle your rebel-lions
on the One-Hearted Vision
of the Dawn

Cry out in the night to remind us
Remember us in your tears and shadows
Brush up against us with your moving limbs
So we quiver again

Let your milk and honey
flow through this Promised Land

# BOOK TWO
# INITIATION

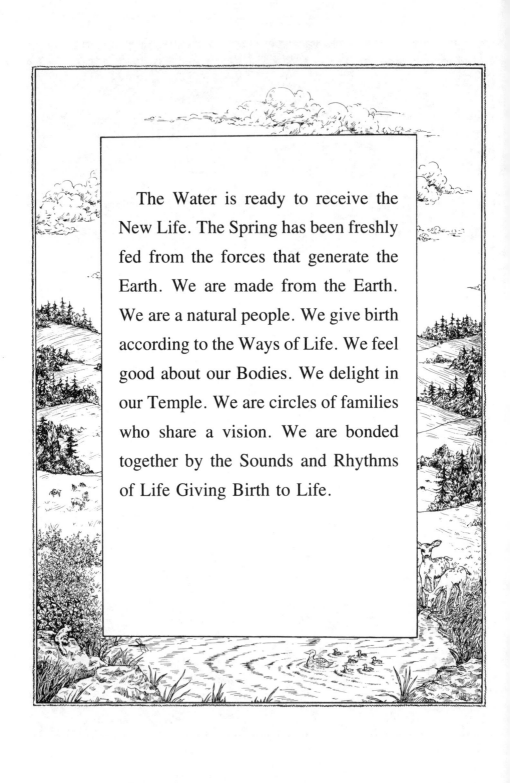

The Water is ready to receive the New Life. The Spring has been freshly fed from the forces that generate the Earth. We are made from the Earth. We are a natural people. We give birth according to the Ways of Life. We feel good about our Bodies. We delight in our Temple. We are circles of families who share a vision. We are bonded together by the Sounds and Rhythms of Life Giving Birth to Life.

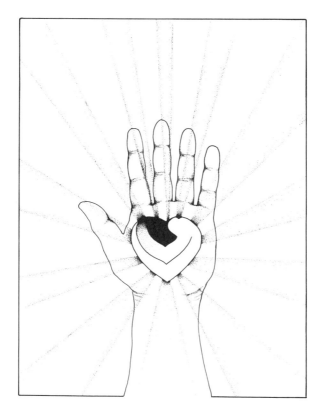

# CHAPTER FOUR

# BIRTHING AND BONDING
## Nature is the Guide

After the conception the Soul lives in the valley in the center of the Universe. We all come from this traceless place where consciousness flows in a vital stream - from the One to the One. Even before the egg is fertilized, before anybody rises in love, the Soul is held in Creation by a Golden-Spirit-Thread. Human beings are held to this earth by the force of Creation. We belong to this ground. Even death does not take us from the earth for long. We return again and again to bond and love.

The Golden-Spirit-Thread turns into the umbilical cord when it is time for us to return to earth. All human beings need love the strongest when they first emerge from the Womb. But the need for love never goes away. The need to be bonded to someone who unconditionally loves you does not atrophy with age.

## Birthing and Bonding

The need for unconditional love must be fulfilled while in the Body. This is what we are here for. There is simply no other reason to subject ourselves to the fire were it not for the flame. The Light of Love draws us to earth to dance and sing. The Light of Love draws us to earth to feel joy and gratitude. Truly there is no greater privilege than to be born again.

A healthy mother feels a strong psychic connection with her babe in the early months of pregnancy. She carries on internal conversations with her child which become more involved as the kicks of the little one increase in magnitude. Fathers also bond with their babes while they are still in the womb. Many fathers have told me of their joy in stroking their mate's naked belly and whispering love songs and prayers to the child inside. The family that consciously bonds with their babe while still in the womb prepares itself for the intensely physical transition from womb to planet earth. Thus intrauterine rapport can easily flow into the caressing, cooing, eyeing, cuddling, and kissing which initiate the parenting instinct.

I asked Nan Koehler-Solomon, author of *Artemis Speaks*, my birthing teacher, to share some of her observations on bonding. In our first interview she told me the story of how she got interested in the whole issue surrounding natural birth and bonding.

I first became interested in natural childbirth to have a healthy baby. I was completely motivated for the welfare of the child. I had heard that drugs weren't good for the baby, so to me it was out of the question to use drugs.

Having the baby at home was a purely accidental phenomenon. And then I experienced the bonding and I said, "Holy God, what a difference!" I had a much closer relationship with my home-born child than with my hospital-born one. Everybody said, "Oh, it's just because of the way you birthed it," and that wasn't it. It's because I got the *biological trigger into the phenomena which you don't have when your baby comes out and you can't smell it and it's not wet on you.* You have to smell it. *That triggers the maternal instinct* in the lower brain centers and makes you connected with the child. Nothing else can. It's completely olfactory. It's not visual. We live in a visually-oriented society and *you think if you look at the baby through the window you're going to bond, but that's not the way you bond. It's a sensory phenomenon. Touch and smell.* Smell is the predominant one. And then feeling it.

Since then Nan has served the needs of thousands of women and children. Her husband, Dr. Donald Solomon, is a third generation obstetrician and one of the few doctors in the nation who comprehend what giving birth is all about. Together they facilitate the Rainbow Birthing Center. Recently Nan helped a young couple who were having a hard time having a baby. When I told her to tell me more about bonding she told me their story:

A recent experience has led me to believe that the quality of the extended postpartum experience, and not just the bonding at birth, is a deciding factor in getting families off to a truly good start. A woman in our community birthed under general anesthesia with an emergency caesarean for a prolapsed cord. Her pediatrician overreacted to the baby's slight malformations (a cleft lip and mild hypospadias). The mother was so traumatized by the birth that she did not even want to see the baby at first. Luckily, we were there to help her over the "hump" of those first few hours postpartum.

The baby nursed well, and the mother's reserves began to melt. However, two weeks after the birth, the baby was slightly jaundiced and hadn't regained the pound he had lost since his birth. This galvanized me and the other women in my community to rally around the mother. We had been bringing her food, but now I checked her every day, with attention to every detail of how the baby was doing. We told her daily how beautiful she was and what a good job she was doing  and how wonderful her baby was. They were truly a Madonna and child. The growth of their relationship and the development of the baby after this was stunning. Today, at eight weeks postpartum, both look fantastic. We even stopped weighing the baby weekly because he is obviously growing!

What happened with this mother? As I see it, two main factors contributed to the dramatic improvement in the child. First, the mother stayed home exclusively with the baby, in a quiet environment. Secondly, she benefited from the intense witness/support of other experienced nursing mothers.

Most other cultures take care of this automatically with their taboos and so-called superstitions. In truth, they support the interests of Mother Nature by having prescribed periods of isolation and social deprivation as well as food regulations. (Only certain people can see the baby: Father, Grandmother, Aunt, etc., but *not* strangers.) In India, for example, the new mother and baby stayed in a darkened room for some time, with only candle light. Of course, they take the baby outside periodically during the day, but the idea is to rest the baby's eyes and create a safe, stimulus-free environment. Most American Indian people, whom I've read about, have a two-week period of isolation with the baby, often spent in a darkened room. At the end of that time, a ceremony is held introducing the baby to the world and dedicating him/her to the earth. In the Middle East and much of Asia, the isolation time is even longer. Forty days are spent in one's room with the baby. All household chores are done by someone else during this time. An anthropologist, Dana Raphael, has written a wonderful book on this subject, called *The Tender Gift*.

By way of example, let me tell you about my birth experiences. I had no trouble giving birth to my first child; it was in a hospital setting with minimal interference of any sort. I was very proud of my six-hour first labor! But that experience didn't bring me the personal transformation that my second (home) birth did. My relationship with the two babies was also very different. As I wrote earlier, I attributed my different reactions to the setting and to the intensity of the bonding experience. In the bright hospital room the baby was caught by the Doctor, handed to a nurse who weighed, measured, dried and foot-printed the baby (while the Doctor stitched the episiotomy) and then handed it back to me wrapped in a blanket.

In the darkened room at home, my mate caught the baby and immediately handed him to me. I nursed him right away and moved about freely because I didn't tear, and felt normal in every way. In hindsight, I can see that, in fact, the more intense bonding I experienced with my second child was due not only to the more intimate birth setting but also because I was in my Mother's home! She and several friends nurtured me for about eight weeks, until I moved back to California. All that time I didn't have to worry about anything except my baby and my older child. It was a blissful time for me.

In our culture, we aren't careful with our new babies at all. Beginning with birth, strangers touch the infant almost at will and we expose them to frightening sights and sounds. For example, one often hears young couples proclaim that their baby loves to ride in the car and falls right to sleep. The reason they fall asleep is because they experience sensory overload and have to shut it off. The same is true for meetings, shopping, etc., with a newborn. If you're lucky, they'll sleep the whole time you are out (or fuss so much you can't even go out!) But then upon returning home, they are hungry, wet, needing to defecate, etc. — in short, screaming, while you are exhausted from being out all day. This cycle results in colic.

It's better to stay home with the newborn. For how long? It's best to take your cue from the child. Some need more time than others to integrate what is going on around them, or as Joseph Chilton Pearce says in his book, *The Magical Child*, they need more time to bond on the mother. This bonding on the mother can only occur as the result of days on end of total attention to the child. The isolation period varies from culture to culture and it varies from child to child.

In the biology books it says that sometime around *ten weeks* of age the fouva matures. This is the area of the retina where the rods and cones are most densely concentrated. When this happens, one definitely notices a marked change in the child. Suddenly, they're interested in what is going on around them. They aren't so preoccupied with their own internal rumblings. Some children can branch out earlier, while others need more time getting used to their body. My last child (my fifth) didn't like going out at all until very recently. She is nine months old!

The biological results of this isolation are a tranquil child and an intense telepathic relationship between mother and child. The social results of adhering to a period of isolation are manifold and healing to the family. With the mother home constantly, a stable base is established for the rest of the family. This source of emotional stability and comfort is underestimated by our culture. One can't create a home via interior decorating and arriving at the door at 5 p.m. It takes time and attention to see to all the details of creating a loving space.

Another benefit from this isolation and intense bonding is a baby who is very comfortable with its bodily functions. Alone with mom all this time, its physical needs met promptly and without haste, the child grows accustomed to eating, sleeping, urinating, defecating, burping, etc., with no trauma. The long-term benefit is a child in tune with his/her body and able to look after him/herself intuitively at a later age.

Here is the format that my circle of women friends and I have developed in the last few years to heal and support our families.

1.   *The waxing moon before the woman is due, give her a Blessing Way.*

2.   *Support the woman in whatever birth choice/place is appropriate for her, then have her stay in bed the first week after her baby's birth, except for going to the bathroom. The new mother should drink lots of comfrey tea (two pots a day at least), take her vitamins, drink a quart of carrot juice each day, etc. With different women friends bringing dinner each night, the husband doesn't need to worry about the evening meal.*

## Birthing and Bonding

*If desired, this support woman can do a few simple chores — laundry, dishwashing, etc. — but most couples like to be left alone. If someone can come stay in the home in a discreet way and serve the new mother, that's even more desirable.*

*3. The second week after the birth, the mother can be up, but resting and definitely at home. The suppers from friends should continue for another week.*

*4. At the end of two weeks, the midwife or support person should come and give the mother an herbal bath, review with her how to massage her baby and lead the family in a ceremony celebrating the safe passage and introducing the new child to the earth forces. Thus we dedicate the child to the healing of our earth and the strengthening of the new family. The Blessing Way beforehand and this ceremony afterward serve to remind us of our higher goals.*

*5. Remember that six weeks after birth is the low point. If one can pass this time without getting sick, that is a feat and a real measure of how well this isolation was handled.*

In summary, the time alone with a beautiful, innocent-but crabby, up-at-night, often with inexplicable aches and pains baby, has many benefits. The major benefit, not mentioned yet, is to the woman herself. Dealing with a being who is not interested in anything external, but who needs constant input, without anger or frustration, is a feat of maturity. People pay money to go on retreats where they can't sleep, must fast, etc., to enter the state that all nursing mothers who take loving care of their babies are in. The combination of sleep deprivation and constant selfless service taken in stride with grace and humor prepare the woman for any challenge in later life. And so we see that the skills gained during this period help her become a source of strength for her whole community.

■    ■    ■

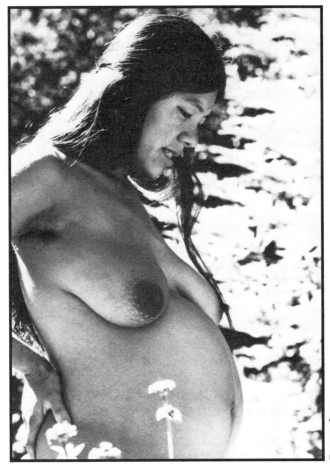

Forrest Jang

*The work of the teacher is not to teach balance, the work is to teach qualities; life will bring about balance by itself, as long as boys and girls are taught that particular quality which belongs to them.* —Hazrat Inayat Khan

Initiation 55

## Home-Birth Preparations

All birth is Holy, all babies Divine. Wherever a babe is born is Holy ground. All methods are secondary to the Spirit. Holy is birth. God protects the babe from all "methods" of birth.

With the return of the midwife has come an expanded range of options in the birthing experience. In the last ten years, a wide range of new birthing ways has been developed to facilitate the well-being of mother and child.

I asked Marilyn Murphy, a midwife friend, to share some of her observations of the current trends in natural childbirth.

Birth is a sacred rite. Many of those whom I serve feel this very deeply and cannot allow their sacred rite of passage to be dictated by hospital protocol. For this, and many other reasons, the home birth movement is growing.

Many women feel that they cannot relax in a foreign environment like the hospital, so they choose to stay at home where they feel safer and more able to loosen up and let the baby out. Hospital obstetric floors are not really conducive to the very private, primal, sensual and spiritual experience that birth is! Some women insist on birthing at home because they are intent upon having older siblings witness the birth (and this is often contrary to hospital policy). For many of us, birthing at home is a natural outgrowth of reclaiming our power, taking control of our lives, and bringing birth back to the family.

For many women, it is their desire to be cared for by a midwife, instead of a doctor, which compels them to birth at home. Midwives, both lay and certified, are more apt to feel comfortable allowing the normal processes of labor and birth to unfold. Doctor's training tends to lean more toward pathology and intervention. Many people believe that a home birth is safer than a hospital birth because there is less chance of incurring problems from obstetrical intervention and no risk of hospital-caused infection.

Although hospital birth is the current obstetrical standard for safe birth in this country, the scientific literature does not prove hospital birth to be safer. *The Five Standards for Safe Childbirth*, by David Stewart, Ph.D., cites good nutrition, skillful midwifery, natural childbirth, homebirth, and breastfeeding as the hallmarks of a truly safe childbearing, and gives hundreds of references to validate this stance.

Hospital "alternative birth rooms," where women can labor and birth in a bedroom-type setting, and freestanding alternative birth centers are recent attempts to find compromises between home and hospital birthings.

Prenatal preparation and education are invaluable for the woman desiring a natural childbirth with a good outcome. A real understanding of pregnancy and birth demystifies the process and can help eliminate fears. A variety of childbirth classes offer childbirth education and preparation for labor and birth.

There are several commonly used coping styles which a woman may use to help herself relax during her labor and allow her body to open up. Attention to breathing and specific breathing techniques can help a woman keep her focus and stay loose during contractions.

Most women benefit immensely with a labor coach to help them with their breathing and remind them to stay relaxed during contractions. Good womanly support is so important. How reassuring for the laboring woman to look into the eyes of one who has already done it!

*Bradley Method childbirth* classes teach techniques for total relaxation and use slow deep breathing during labor and birth. The entire body remains calm and relaxed as if asleep, and the slow, deep breathing assures that the mother and baby are well supplied with oxygen.

*Lamaze Method childbirth* classes teach deep relaxation, with a gradual quickening and lightening of the breathing as contractions increase in intensity.

Both methods are very effective and some women use a combination of breathing styles over the course of their labor. Some women invent their own breathing styles quite naturally. Whatever works! The trick is to stay really relaxed even during the most intense contractions. Tension and fear can interfere with the natural progress of labor.

Keeping the mouth loose helps make the cervix loose and aids dilation (opening). French kissing is good for this! Or making deep, open sounds. Some women find their way through their labors via womansong: improvising with their own unique sounds and chants.

There is no one ''right'' way to deal with the bittersweet pain of labor. It is good to prepare by practicing relaxation techniques throughout pregnancy and learning some breathing techniques to try. Those attending the birth can use hot baths, massage, and acupressure to deepen the relaxation of the laboring woman.

Finally, we realize that we don't have to lie on a labor bed and scream for painkillers! It is possible to experience labor sensations totally, from a calm and centered place, and even possible to enjoy the process of naturally opening to birth with all its incredible intensity. Birthing this way is empowering and life-changing each time it happens.

Recent research is verifying what some of us have known for ages: the newborn is very sensitive, intelligent, receptive and aware being. In light of this, parents and birth attendants are creating birthing environments with the intent of affecting the newborn in the most positive ways.

*Dr. Frederick Leboyer*, of France, developed a birthing method to ease the transition from womb-world to this world. Babies are born into a quiet, dimly-lit birthing room and immediately placed in a warm bath. The new-born is gently supported as s/he floats and uncurls and stretches in the water for a gentle welcoming. Leboyer describes this type of birth in his book, *Birth Without Violence*. A home birth adaption of the Leboyer method could be a small tub beside the birthing bed or even a clean bathtub. A "Leboyer" birth is a welcome alternative to the cold delivery room with glaring lights.

■　■　■

**Underwater birthing** is one of the most radically innovative birthing methods happening to date. Mothers labor in a tank or pool of warm water, and babies are born into the water and may remain submerged for a period of minutes. Babies do not attempt to breathe underwater as long as the water temperature of the tank approximates the womb temperature and they are still receiving oxygen through the umbilical cord. These babies are born from the waters of the womb, through the birth canal, to the larger waters outside — a gentle transition. Generally, these infants appear calm and untraumatized by the birth.

I have attended one underwater birth and can testify to its magic. In this instance the woman was forty-three years old, a mother of three, and a grandmother. The birth took place in the bathtub of a friendly neighbor. She had not planned to have an underwater birth. But when the time came to birth she did not feel at ease in her own home. So she went next door and found the most comfortable place in her friend's home: the bathroom.

When we arrived she was in the tub. We turned that bathroom into a Holy Space. We prayed and called in the Great Spirit of Life. The birth happened with ease. There were no complications.

Jeannine Parvati's fifth child was born underwater. She sent me this story about her experience. It is a most beautiful description of giving birth.

*Babies have never been a logical choice in my life. I HEAR THE CALL OF THE CHILD SOMEWHERE BETWEEN ESTROGEN AND PROGESTERONE AND BEGIN THE DIALOG.*

*"I NEED MORE TIME," my first opening. "THERE IS NO SUCH THING AS TIME HERE" the spirit voice, or pre-baby answers. From the soul's point of view there is no time. That is how hours can be spent in daydream (lifetimes actually) and it seems like an instant.*

*"We can't afford another baby,"* the rational, accountant mind responds. *"I am coming to you not for what you will buy me"* counters the pre-babe.

*"I do already love you."* My heart softens the edges of my mind. The argument is weakening. *"My intention is not to make you poor, but to enrich your life beyond your hopes. I AM COMING TO SHOW YOU WHAT YOUR LOVE LOOKS LIKE."*

Change is afoot in many ways. We move our entire home business from Utah to Hawaii for the pregnancy. Gestating in the tropical rain forest without creature comforts of civilization, and lots of jungle creatures. Since we had no electricity, it was to bed when the sun goes down and up just before dawn. We breathe clean Pacific Ocean air. We swim in crystal blue ocean and drink pure rainwater. In Hawaii I grow to love water and often imagine when floating in the ocean and riding waves, that I am like my baby now, surrounded and sustained by salty water. Along the way we discover that paradise is a state of mind.

While in Hawaii, I attend midwife meetings and learn about under-water birth. THERE IS A RICH HERITAGE OF BIRTHING TIDEPOOLS FOR THE ISLANDERS. I hear about the Australian, the French, and Russian women who birth their babies underwater for millenia. There are stories about dolphins being midwives to women birthing. I am more than intrigued – I AM ATTRACTED TO THIS CONCEPT BEYOND LOGIC, JUST AS I WAS OPEN TO THE FIFTH BABY FOR REASONS BEYOND "COMMON SENSE."

I have no fear of birth. That's a gift, as well as an earned trust. From the moment the bloody show came, I knew our baby would arrive within several hours. All my other babies had been born on the full moon (or within hours). How did I know the delivery would be perfect? The same way I knew that I was pregnant so early on. The brain-heart knows. And once the monkey-mind quiets down enough, all the information we need is right here, within.

This is my first labor in the daytime. All four babies had initiated their labors at midnight and come before or just at dawn. IT SEEMED SO NAKED, SO OBVIOUS TO GIVE BIRTH IN THE DAYTIME. I SUBMERGE ALL MODESTY AND GIVE MYSELF TO BIRTH.

Being the empiricist that I am, I must try the various stages of labor in and out of the water bath. Does the water really help? In earlier labor there seemed to be little difference. Except that I can more easily kiss and hug my family on dry land than in our tiny bathtub. But once we move towards transition, I note a marked change out of the water. The gifts become LABOR PAINS, out of the bath, while in the warm water the birthforce JUST FEELS STRONG. Even up to the second stage I am get-

*ting in and out of the tub to feel the difference. Each time I carefully wash my feet to keep the water clean. Oh yes, THE WATER DEFINITELY HELPS TRANSFORM PAIN INTO URGENT PRESSURE.*

*I feel the baby come down. The sensation is ecstatic. I had prepared somewhat for this being painful as my last delivery had been. Yet this time the pulse of birth feels wonderful! I am building up to the birth climax and with one push the babe is in canal. THE NEXT PUSH BRINGS HIM DOWN, DOWN INTO THAT SPACE JUST BEFORE ORGASM WHEN WE WOMEN KNOW HOW GOD MUST HAVE FELT CREATING THIS PLANET.*

*The water supports my birth outlet. I AM NO LONGER AN ISLAND ALONE IN THIS WORK. I FEEL CONNECTED TO THE MAINLAND, TO MY SOURCE. THESE MIDWIFE HANDS KNOW JUST WHAT TO DO TO SUPPORT THE NOW CROWNING HEAD, coming so fast. How glad I am for all those years of orgasms! Slow orgasms, fast ones, those which build and subside and peak again and again. That practice aids my baby's gentle emergence so that he doesn't spurt out too quickly. HE COMES, AS I DO.*

*I slip my fingers around his neck, and what's this? Ah, a little hand. I hold back this hand as he rotates and delivers first one shoulder, then the other. OUT SLIPS OUR BABY INTO HIS PARENT'S HANDS. HE SWIMS RIGHT INTO OUR HEARTS.*

*Some "water babies" stay submerged after delivery for a few minutes but mine wants to come to the surface immediately. He turns and faces me, eyes shut, and says - "Lift me up!"*

*I pull my baby up to the surface and drape a towel over his head. Gradually he opens one eye, then the other to gaze in wonder. He isn't breathing perceptively so I hug him all the closer and sing the welcoming song. He is warm and the color is coming on so I do not worry as we await his first perceptible breath. I kiss his face, gently sucking out the mucus in his airways through nose and mouth. We ADORE him.*

*The placenta, or the "Grandmother" as we like to call the baby's first mother, delivers itself minutes later. How easy clean-up is when birthing in the bathtub! Most all the blood clots fall to the bottom of the tub, whose water is bright red now. I RECALL THE STORY OF MOSES AND THE PARTING OF THE RED SEA. MY POST-PARTUM BODY FEELS AS IF MOSES HAD JUST BEEN THROUGH WITH THE CHOSEN ONES.*

*The first few days earthside we watch carefully for any signs of infection. We had heard about a few post-partum fevers in underwater birthings. I take my favorite herbal antibiotic ally, echinacea root, in tincture. I feel terrific. The only problem was slight constipation in my nursing baby - a side effect of echinacea. During the birth I had defecated just a little bit into the water and wanted to play it safe in case some E. Coli, etc., had found its way into my uterus. Now Quinn is 11 months old and neither of us have shown any signs of bacterial infection.*

*WAS IT THE WATER WHICH MADE THIS BIRTH SO ECSTATIC AND SEXUALLY FULFILLING? I would like to shout, "IT'S THE WATER!" but must admit, only possibly so. It is alot easier for me to interpret the birthforce as blissful rushes when they don't hurt. Yet in all honesty, I don't really know for sure. This is the way it is with birth - it doesn't lend itself to repeatable experiment well. Each birth is totally unique. I just remember that when Quinn came into my birth canal there was no way I would forsake the warm comfort of the bath.*

■   ■   ■

## Lotus Birth

With the Lotus Birth, we have the opportunity to focus our attention on the placenta in a new way. In the Lotus Birth, the umbilical cord is left uncut and allowed to atrophy and fall away on its own. In a sense, the Lotus Birth is an over-compensation for insensitive birthing practices. It is a reaction to the routine and systematic denial of bonding which has been the standard birth protocol for so many years. It is a physical way to protect the bonding process. By not immediately cutting the cord, the Divine connection between mother and child is protected.

In some rural and tribal settings, such a practice may be physically unfeasible or offensive to tradition. The length of the mother's labor may also be a factor in deciding how to treat the placenta. She may need to eat the placenta for her own strength and well-being, (from exhaustion or after excessive blood loss, for example).

Claire Day, the leading proponent for the Lotus Birth, offers her perspective:

The placenta is a one-to-one mediator for child and mother. It is very auspicious. Reverence and care of the placenta is a family affair. While the cord is drying up, and the placenta also, for the first 24 hours it is wise to keep the cord level while the baby is at rest and sleeping. The placenta, being the highest vibratory-rate organ of the whole body and very close to the central spiritual sun, is kept level with the cord. As the child breathes, the cord constricts and will dry up.

## Birthing and Bonding

A pyramid (bedside) can be placed over the placenta to aide in curing, dehydrating it, and keeping the odor down. The pyramid is not an absolute necessity, but an aide. Another aide is a blue light bulb, which can be shined for 15 minutes a day on the placenta for subtleness and to keep odor down. Eucalyptus leaves and buds, cedar leaves, and such clean-smelling things can be placed around the placenta. Put auspicious things near it too. I have used gold, lapis, precious uncut whole stones, gems, flowering plants, and herbs (in pots—do not bring cut flowers around; this is a reminder of what has been done to our center, the umbilical cord, for centuries). We are starting a wholistic, healthy spiritual practice, simple and clean.

The placenta can dry also by the sun. If you are fortunate enough to have a flower garden, and it is warm, sun baby outside, wrap the placenta in a clean cloth, and use the availability of God's colors.

■　　■　　■

I have only been to one lotus birth. On the day of the birth Nan and I went for a long walk with the mother and father. We all bathed in the cool waters of a stream. After the walk the couple went home and rested. I went over to their house around seven in the evening. The midwives expected the birth to happen soon. But it didn't. The mother would not be rushed. She knew exactly how she wanted her birth to be.

Dorothea, the mother, asked me to play my drum. I played for a while and stopped. She told me to either play or leave. So I got up and took a walk. When I came back the room was real quiet and practically everyone had left. The vibes felt really nice. I picked up Nan's drum and it was just right. It played me. I started to sing a song about Jesus and Mary Magdalene. As soon as I started singing the waters broke. The birth was bliss. Total. Complete. Dorothea felt no pain. She enjoyed herself immensely.

She decided to do a Lotus birth because she felt it was a matter of principle to begin her chilld's life with as little violence as possible. I asked her to tell us about her experience with the lotus birth.

To lotus birth is to complete the natural process of relaxed, peaceful birthing by allowing the umbilical cord to break forth from the navel in its own time. The placenta is bathed and kept swathed in clean, dry cloth.

After a blissful and relaxed birthing I chose to allow my fourth baby to experience a lotus birth because anything less would have seemed harsh and interruptive. Even the most peace-filled birth is still a shock. The cutting and clamping of the cord create an aura of tension which the simple wrapping of the placenta avoids.

In the first days after birth, this connection provides an extra incentive for the mother to slow down, which is especially important if it is not her first born. Also, although the placenta does not provide physical nourishment it has a subtle psychic effect. I grew to love the placenta and encouraged my whole family to do likewise.

On the fourth day when the cord released, both Michelle and I felt a brief sense of loss, and then elation with each other as another stage in the bonding process began. In the days and weeks that followed I felt a strength and vitality that had not occurred with my other three children.

I recommend lotus birth for those who are ready to take a giant leap. It opens the gateway for wisdom and blessings. Yet the blessing is only sustained by regular, daily prayer and constant attunement to the Divine within.

■　　■　　■

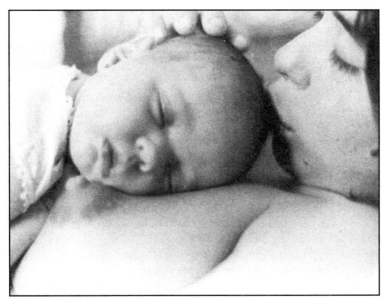

Brian Cook

## Breastfeeding

Breastfeeding teaches the nursing child the qualities of One-Heart. It is on Mother's breast that we learn the self-awareness that makes us human. Nursing is one of the most rewarding experiences on this planet. The newborn who is breastfed exhibits a peacefulness not seen in bottle-fed babies. This is an indication of not only better digestion, but also of an emotional rapport between mother and baby. Intelligent breastfeeding promotes self-reliance and independence in the child.

The most important ingredient of mother's milk is Love. But breastmilk is also the freshest, most economical, tastiest, best-suited food for the human infant. It is clean and "certified raw." It is served at the ideal temperature. It is the only food which is conducive to the optimal development of the glands and organs of the human body.

Only through nursing does the baby receive colostrum, a yellowish pre-milk secretion which contains essential antibodies. The laxative effect of colostrum helps baby pass meconium from his/her intestine. Mother's milk is rich in Vitamin E. The nucleic acid balance is perfect for the mineral composition of human tissue. The amino acid ratio is perfect for building the sensitive tissue of the nervous system.

Breastmilk is the only food that produces comparatively odorless, non-irritating, soft stools. It is the only food that gives baby a sweet breath and perspiration. The breastfed baby's urine will not scald its tender skin.

We have much work to do to protect the new mother and child. The centralized arm of chemical medicine, doctors in hospitals, must be prevented from drying up the milk. The white frocked priests have been duped by the formula salesmen. But technology can never duplicate mother's milk. It cannot even come close. The living element will always be missing. The spark of life will never be there.

Formulas based on cow's milk are deficient in Vitamin E and K. Mother's milk can be rich in these nutrients provided the mother has a good diet. A healthy woman has friendly bacteria to produce Vitamin K. The B vitamin content of mother's milk will increase with the use of whole grain, raw seeds and nuts, and nutritional yeast.

Little iron is found in either breast milk or cow's milk. That supplied in breastmilk, however, is absorbed far more efficiently than the iron in cow's milk. If the mother's prenatal diet has been adequate, a full-term baby has stored enough iron to last for six months. Researchers now believe that if the nursing mother's diet is rich enough in iron, supplementation to the child is unnecessary.

Breastmilk offers more readily absorbed nutrients, and is more digestible than cow's milk or formula. The fat globules in cow's milk are larger than those in breastmilk and therefore are more difficult to digest.

But outweighing any comparisons of breastmilk to other kinds of food for the infant is the knowledge that a suckling babe is the true expression of that deep connection between mother and child. As that truth is affirmed with each nursing, both babe and mother are nourished. As one mother puts it: "We're in love!"

*A major biochemical difference between human milk and formula is the cholesterol content. Human milk contains 20 mg. cholesterol per 100 ml.; the cholesterol concentrations of the three most widely used formulas range from 1.5 to 3.3 mg. per 100 ml. The amount of cholesterol needed by infants has not been established, but judging from several animal studies, infants may require a moderate amount of dietary cholesterol to establish mechanisms for proper metabolism of cholesterol in later life. These studies involved feeding infant rats and weaning rats varying amounts of cholesterol. One study showed that male rats fed a low-cholesterol diet in infancy had higher serum cholesterol levels when older than those initially fed diets containing moderate amounts of cholesterol. In another study, male rats prematurely weaned to a cholesterol-free diet had elevated blood cholesterol levels later in life. These research findings imply that low-cholesterol formulas may contribute to atherosclerosis, one of the our most serious health problems.*

*Additional biochemical differences exist between human milk and formulas. Human milk contains a rich supply of nucleotides, substances involved in protein and nucleic acid synthesis. The distribution of amino acids differs considerably. The fatty acid composition of human milk substitutes varies appreciably from that of human milk, and lipase, an enzyme that enhances availability of free fatty acids, is present in large quantities only in human milk.*

White Paper on Infant Feeding Practices

# Birthing and Bonding

*What about the fear that the child who nurses for several years will become a homosexual? The theory behind it is that the prolonged nursing relationship will make a boy too dependent and therefore effeminate. But what about girls? They are purported to be at risk too. Does their dependency result in too much feminine behavior too? Is that the definition of a Lesbian woman, one who is too feminine? They can't both be true and there is every reason to believe that both of these theses are false, but they continue to crop up and worry mothers who are trying to do their best for their children.*

*Early in my career as a La Leche League leader, I realized just how far some of the "experts" will go to support those beliefs. At a meeting one mother of a 17-month old nursing child brought up her recent visit with the pediatrician. He ordered her to stop nursing on pain of causing homosexuality in her child. "If he had been a girl" the doctor said, "it would be different, but it is very dangerous to continue nursing a boy so long." In her heart, this mother knew something was wrong, but she was genuinely worried nonetheless, until a second mother told the same story with an important difference. Her child was a girl. To no one's surprise, the myth-maker was the same pediatrician. It was a good lesson in exercising common sense, in trusting one's own instincts and perceptions of one's child.*

Elizabeth Hormann, *Mothering Magazine,* Spring '82

Michael Michaelis

## The Family Bed

*Breastfeeding mothers may have noticed that not infrequently they will awaken in the middle of the night shortly before their baby begins to whimper. Results of recent research suggest, according to an article in an LLLI (La Leche League International) publication, that a nursing mother may awake in anticipation of her child's cry because she and her infant dream in unison. It is suspected that the hormone prolactin may be the key to this mysterious link. This lasts for only as long as breastfeeding is continued. With bottlefed infants and their mothers this will last only for about two weeks. After that, mother and child have completely different and unequal sleep cycles.*

Tine Thevenin
The Family Bed, *pg. 101*

The assumption that children should not be around at night is one that is certainly not made by the nursing mother. For her, having baby close allows a good night's sleep. Otherwise, she must get up and go to another room to respond to a crying and already cranky child. Indeed, when mother and child sleep side-by-side, Mother's let-down response corresponds exactly to the child's nursing needs.

The mother has an instinct to stay close to her child. But this instinct has been misinterpreted by patriarchal analysis. We have been warned that letting our children too close to the bedroom is dangerous. (Obviously, this advice has not produced a well-adjusted sexual character: one in four female children is sexually molested by a male relative.)

When newborns snuggle close to their mother and father, they feel the warmth, security, and comfort of love. Within each child is a deep need to surrender to and be accepted in, a bond of unconditional love. Every newborn wants to sleep as close as possible to his/her parents. Every newborn has an internal antenna lovingly zeroed-in on Mother's umbilicus. This antenna is a psychic cord with more accuracy than radar. This connection is a continuation of the bond which began in the womb with the umbilical cord. This connection predates the development of the Self. It occurs when the Self and the Universe are one pulsating unit.

The family bed is a bed where children and parents sleep together. If one thinks in conventional terms, the family bed seems highly impractical. It challenges conventional notions about parental privacy, especially sexual privacy. It demands a reordering of priorities within the home. But the family bed *is* practical, not only for the nursing mother, but also for working fathers who want to spend quality time with their children.

The following three stories will explain more about the concept of family bed.

### CHILDREN IN BED WITH MOM AND DAD

When I had my first child, 15 years ago, my major input regarding ideas about child-rearing were the Gerber Baby Foods ads and my mother's Germanic/scientific concepts of baby care. I thought babies slept most of the time and only needed to be fed, changed and put back to sleep. I didn't realize that they needed to be cuddled, talked to, stimulated and included in *my* life. I envisioned having a baby as being kind of like getting a puppy or kitten! My ignorance wasn't unique because I've read about, observed and spoken with many women having the same experience.

Luckily, this child, my son, is a Leo with Aries rising and a Virgo moon (strong-willed, fussy, colicky, very intelligent, extroverted and constantly in search of stimuli) so there was no way I could impose this artificial vision on him. He kept waking up at night any old time he felt like it; he never slept more than 45 minutes during the daytime and wanted to be entertained and stimulated constantly. He didn't enjoy just hanging out nursing, as my daughters did, so I couldn't get much reading done. Oh how I had to learn to surrender! Whenever I tried to get him to sleep longer or to sleep in his space (a crib in the corner) by letting him cry, for example, he would develop sniffles. The connection was obvious. In the same vein, he wouldn't let me force-feed him beginning at 3 months old with applesauce as my "doctor" had advised.

I don't remember how long it took me (it seemed like an eternity, maybe 2-3 months) but by the time he was 4 months old, I had figured out the "lay of the land." One morning when he was up for his 5 a.m. feeding (which happened in the rocking chair next to his bed), I gave up trying to cajole him into sleeping some more in his crib so that I could go back to bed as well. What bliss for us both when, in great fatigue, I just dragged him from across the room and we snuggled together and dozed while he sucked. It took me a while, but I learned to sleep while he nursed.

*Don't think I had learned my lesson.* It took two more children to really teach me it was okay to keep the baby in bed with me. The difficulty came for me because sleeping with my children didn't fit my image of what one did with a baby and I didn't know anyone else who did that sort of thing. My husband was completely nonplussed. Slowly, with more reading (my favorite books are Sheila Kippley's *Breastfeeding and*

## Birthing and Bonding

*Natural Childspacing* and Tine Thevenin's *The Family Bed*), doing affir-
mations and especially watching the results of my early ignorance—my
oldest boy sucked his thumb and clung to his security blanket until he
was over 9 years old—I didn't care anymore what anyone thought or
said. I wanted my babies in bed with me for as long as they wanted to be
there. When else can one hug someone and be hugged 24 hours a day!
This attitude takes away the anguish and fatigue of early infancy.

Love — Nan

## OUR FAMILY BED

My son, Jeremiah, was born at home in a very gentle and loving way.
On a warm October morning he came on rhythmic waves, easing slowly
into the world. I reached down and pulled him up onto my bare belly. We
fell in love. His eyes looked into mine as I took him to my breast and we
melted together. He never left my side. For three months, we were
always together. We slept together at night and I had him and carried
him around with me all day.

It wasn't long before we fell into a comfortable nursing pattern. He
would nurse 2-5 times a night and about every two hours during the day.
I often napped with him during the day in order to stay well rested. At
first I would sit up at night to nurse him. After awhile I figured out how to
nurse him laying down and I would drift in and out of sleep as he nursed.
This interrupted sleeping pattern allowed me to get in better touch with
my dreams. I soon learned to appreciate the alpha state this type of nursing allowed me to experience. It was so much nicer than getting up out
of bed every 2-4 hours when my baby was hungry or lonely. Jeremiah
never knew loneliness. He was never left alone crying in a dark and
abandoned room. Whenever he awoke there was always someone
there to greet him and care for him. He was a very happy and secure
baby. He didn't cry as much as other babies his age.

The hardest aspect of sharing my bed with Jeremiah was finding the
time and space to be intimate with his father. Our way of relating was
drastically altered after the birth of our son. We found ourselves
scheduling time to spend together alone. When Jeremiah was older, we
even got him a babysitter one night a week just so we could have dinner
together in peace and be alone. It took us awhile to feel comfortable
making love in front of a sleeping son. Usually he would sleep right
through all the passionate movement. Occasionally he would wake up
and wonder what was going on. I would simply stick my nipple in his
mouth and lay quietly for a few minutes and he would fall back to sleep.
When he got older, like around two, he would want to join in on the ac-

tion and would nurse aggressively until things calmed down. This activity seemed a little strange at first but our lovemaking was always slow and gentle and very loving and I couldn't see how it could hurt him in any way. He quickly learned that this was an act of love and gentle caring.

As he got older, he became less and less interested in watching this loving dance and would either go back to sleep or go into the other room where he had his own bed. Now we even make love during the day and he plays quietly by himself, ignoring us. Sex is not something that is bad or dirty in this house. It is a very special and intimate way to share with the one you love. Intimacy and sexuality have never been hidden from Jeremiah. He is very comfortable with his own sexuality and with any expression of it.

Sharing my bed with Jeremiah has had many benefits. He gets all the loving and cuddling he wants or needs. When he's sick, I can keep a constant monitor on his well-being and make sure he gets the comfort and caring he needs. I don't have to worry about him getting too hot or too cold because I can always feel him right next to me. I don't ever have to worry about him choking or smothering himself. If he's ever feeling sad or insecure I can be right there for him and hold him all night long. And perhaps the most special benefit is that I always awake to a happy smiling face that says "Hi mummies...I love you." That alone is worth any inconvenience that sharing your bed with your child might bring up.

When Jeremiah was around two, he got into the habit of nursing all night long. Whenever anyone in the bed would stir he would wake up and nurse. This became very frustrating for me and I often woke up in the morning totally exhausted. I finally got him a little bed which I placed right next to mine. After I had nursed him to sleep I would put him on his bed and he would sleep much better and for longer periods of time. He could easily crawl into bed with me if he woke up in the middle of the night but he was separate enough that he didn't wake up every time I moved.

*This brings up the issue of weaning.* It is very hard to wean a child from nursing when you sleep with them. Some of the things that worked for us were: letting Jeremiah sleep on his father's side of the bed, wearing a shirt to bed and telling him he couldn't nurse until the sun came up, reading him stories to sleep instead of nursing him to sleep, and then finally getting up first thing in the morning and fixing him breakfast. It was a gradual process taking around three months. But once it was done, he never asked to nurse again.

Jeremiah is almost three now and he has his own room with his own bed. He has the choice to sleep wherever he wants to. I never turn him away from my bed. It seems the more I let him sleep with me the more secure he is about sleeping by himself. Jeremiah is very independent for his age. He's very secure within himself and within our relationship. When I leave him with other people he never cries or fusses about me leaving and always knows I'll come back for him. He plays well with other children as well as adults and often entertains himself for hours. He makes himself at home wherever he goes and is very sociable. I attribute his gentle and loving nature to three things: he was born at home in a gentle way; he was nursed on demand for 2½ years; and he slept in the family bed. He has been a strong teacher for me and a great joy in my life.

Love — Madrone

*Madrone is an educator, ceremonialist, singer, and midwife.*

# A CROSS CULTURAL PERSPECTIVE

When people challenge me on my decision to sleep with my children, I often tell them that this is a common custom in other cultures (I have a B.S. in Cross Cultural Child Development). Some have responded, "But that is only because those people can't afford to give their children separate beds and bedrooms. They would surely choose to sleep separately if they could only afford it." I'm not so sure they would, or that it would be an improvement if they did. A friend of mine tells me of a visitor from Mexico who was shocked to see her baby in a crib. The Mexican woman felt it was cruel and unnecessary. My experience with Costa Rican women, who warned me to keep Arien in a crib, reflects the desire of these people to emulate a Western way of life. They now prefer bottle feeding to breastfeeding, and were shocked at how long I nursed Arien. It isn't always better to do what is "modern" and it is dangerous to equate wealth with "right" or "best."

Western culture has, in the past two or three generations, substituted motherly contact with "things": bottles, cribs, playpens, bouncers, toys...yet none of these can take the place of Mother's attention. And, in society where women are being urged to "make something of themselves," often working outside the home, the family "bed" can provide at least a minimum amount of contact between mother and child or, better yet, Mother, Dad and child. Actually, it isn't so minimal: we spend an average of one third of each day sleeping, and children sleep a few hours longer than adults. Spending that time together, as a "family" is an opportunity for sharing, and caring, that otherwise might just slip past in our highly active, busy lives.

I can't say "it's for everyone" or "it's the best" or that it is a solution to these troubled times. But I can say that, for me and my family, it has been a solution and, for now, feels like the best way for all of us to sleep. It hasn't always been the easiest way for me to sleep, though, and it did take some time adjusting to. There was a time when my son slept restlessly, and would end up with arms and legs stretched over me in the middle of the night. There was also a time when my daughter woke up continuously throughout each night, and friends suggested it was because she slept so close to me. I tried having her sleep separately then, but she woke up even more. It turned out that she was teething, and though it was hard on me, sleep-wise, I'm glad I could offer comfort to her when she needed it.

She needed comforting, too, when I decided to let her "cry it out" for a few days, to cut down on frequent night-nursing, and I'm glad she didn't have to cry all alone, in an isolated bed, let alone in an isolated room. She caught on quickly, and now is content to simply sleep near me, sometimes rolling away to sleep by herself, but then turning to me in the night, and asking that I put my arm around her to "cuddle." ("Cuddle me, Mama...Dere, dat's nice," is our precious nighttime exchange.)

My son enjoys cuddling at bedtime. Sometimes jealous of his nursing sister, he likes to be held close all by himself after she drops off to sleep. In the past, when he slept in his own bed, he often had disturbing dreams. Now he rarely does, but the occasional nightmare is immediately soothed and sorted through, for which I am as grateful as he.

Love — Wendy Sherman

Wendy Sherman is a novelist.

■    ■    ■

*It is a mystery how the white race has come to regard the sexual act which has given life to us and to our children as obscene and unmentionable. If it is something to be ashamed of why do the people who hold such views continue to perform it? And why then did God create the world, according to these people, that this wicked act is absolutely necessary for the procreation of living creatures?*

Elizabeth Haich, Sexual Energy and Yoga

## Circumcision

Circumcision is a mystical ceremony and must be performed by a Holy Man/Woman. The One who makes the incision must keep God's Name resonating constantly. They must consciously meditate upon the Third Eye. On the Eighth Day the pineal gland begins to open to the 'outside Light.' The genitals are directly connected to the Third-Eye-Brain-Center by the spinal fluid. The spinal fluid is referred to in Yogic Texts as the River of Life. This fluid has Three Channels. The central channel is expecially vulnerable during the first year of life.

When the rite is practiced with God Consciousness the baby boy is initiated into Tantra. He learns somatically that the Light in his mind and the power of his loins are One. If the rite is practiced with Holy intention the boy child will emerge from the ceremony keyed into God. He will experience no trauma. Indeed he will feel a sublime joy.

Of course, for most boy babies the operation is far from the sublime. In fact it is an abomination. The original meaning of the ceremony has been lost and the doctors of Babylon have merely added it to their list of money-making necessities. Up until very recently many parents were not even aware that they really had an option. Thankfully thousands of parents every year are beginning to question the need for the "hygienic" operation.

In a New Age what was once done ritualistically is questioned. This is good. Circumcision cuts around the penis but directly interrupts the initial bonding period between mother and child. No other act so ritualistically perpetuates male terror as circumcision. Each time it is performed unconsciously the status quo of patriarchal concensus is upheld.

The best advice I've seen on circumcision came to me in a letter from a new age Rabbi.

*Dear Joshua,*
*I just want to leave you with these thoughts:*
First: *If a parent is not convinced of the covenanting aspect of Bris, but is merely doing the ritual to please the family or for medical purposes, then I advise that they not have their child circumcised.* (Author's note: "Bris" is the Jewish way of circumcision.)

Second: *Even as I advocate Bris as a covenanting ritual (while fully supporting the Lamaze and LeBoyer birthing consciousness), I understand that many sensitive Jewish parents at this point in time, and after serious G-d wrestling on the matter, are choosing not to circumcise their child. Whereas most people with traditional beliefs think this is wrong, I am sympathetic with these parents and see that, in fact, Bris has become for many of us a voluntary, rather than an obligatory, ritual. Seeing circumcision as obligatory is heavy stuff after almost 4,000 years of tradition, I understand all of this in terms of post-holocaust revelation "to turn tradition inside out and re-examine all of the practices and sancta which have been handed down to us." The truth will emerge after a generation. While I firmly believe in this ritual, I am equally adamant in my conviction that we not condemn those who, in full consciousness (and from the depths of their conscience), have decided that they cannot circumcise their child.*

*I know full well most of the counter-arguments, but I still stand by this position.*

*I think we also ought to consider an alternative to the full circumcision we have now and possibly go back to the form used before Hellenistic times.*

*Above all, the method of circumcision used by medical practitioners is an abomination, and under no circumstances would I ever again allow a child of mine to be subjected to this procedure. The only way to go is to find a physician who practices the method of the mohel. The problem is to find one who is not only skilled in his craft, but is conscious of the Lamaze and LeBoyer ways of birthing.*

*For now, Shalom*
*L'Hitraot, Hanan Sills*

*P.S. Under no circumstances should the baby be tied in one of those stupid plastic boards.*

■    ■    ■

The baby boy cannot in any way process the event. The circuits of the nervous system are jammed and emotional balance disrupted. The physical body sends its most resourceful energy to the genitals and soon the intense physical pain subsides and a numbness occurs. If a newly circumcised boy is nursed, the erect nipple restores feeling. The tactile stimulation unifies his oral center. His awareness of Mother helps him forget the pain.

When the baby boy is not nursed, circumcisional pain goes even deeper. No food prepared by the limited wisdom of Betty Crocker or Gerber suits him. The pain in his penis is not alleviated by an attempt to bring him back to life (comfort) with food. When using his mouth in an attempt to restore feeling to his penis doesn't work, he focuses on who is feeding him. Thus food (appetite) and his deep carnal longing for nurturance are at once associated with fear and Her.

Here is a letter from a Mom who consciously struggled with the issue.

*Dear Joshua,*

*I am in love with life and all the wonders that surround me in my small world. My baby boy has doubled in size since birth, so sweet and cute, and I'm blessed with so many little lessons as the mother of sons.*

*When he was born I was surprised to see I'd been sent another boy—and so pleased knowing how perfect God's plan is; we get what we all need.*

*I considered circumcision for only one day; the more I thought about it, the more clear I became that no one was going to take a knife to this little boy! Not while I was alive to protect him.*

*The thing that really clenched it for me was an understanding of the process and what it really involved. I read two very excellent articles, one in Co-Evolution Quarterly and the other in Mothering magazine. It was so scary and graphic and barbaric. What was the purpose?*

*Once my husband and son saw the diagram of what circumcision is, they thought deeply and then neither one fought me on it anymore. I had told my husband that if he were really adamant, to go and watch it being done to some other little boy, and then see if he wanted to watch someone do it to ours. That was it. We were finally clear.*

*Now for my first-born son. His best friend is uncircumcised. Now this little boy is a little spacey when it comes to keeping himself really clean, so I know my son has seen him have some problems with this. That's what my son's opinion on not circumcising was based on. (Actually his friend has gotten it together over the past year.) We have to teach our little boys to keep themselves clean, that's all. It's like remembering to wash behind your ears or wash your armpits, etc.*

*So my son came around to thinking it was okay too. But he made sure, in no uncertain terms, that we know he was glad that he was circumcised — which relieved me of a whole lot of guilt and anguish surrounding his birth and circumcision.*

*Over and over, I've asked myself why I let them take him from me the moment he was born. I got him back 5 hours later. Lord only knows what they did to him. One of those things (or some of those things) made him scream an awful lot the first few weeks of his life. We missed out on that first bonding that is so important. His first experiences were shocking.*

*I was only 18 when my first son was born. I could count the number of cocks I'd ever seen on one hand - all very circumcised. Honestly, I didn't know the difference until I was 25. So when they asked me if I wanted him with skin or without, his father stepped in and said "without." I never questioned it, only out of ignorance and youth. I've grown up a lot.*

*My newborn is a sweet, peaceful baby. I'm convinced that our homebirth experience—a peaceful, loving entry without pain or shock attributes to his smiley face!*

*I realize, also, that we all choose our existence here. My first-born has worked through a lot to be who he is. He's glad—so I've let it go.*

*Love, Sage*
Sage is a dancer

## Making Positive Contact

The way a people give birth and bond is indicative of the way they will do everything else. Because of the terrible derangement in the hospital we have had to create our own life support systems. We have taken back our right to give birth. We are a smarter people now. We are establishing an alternate medical system to which we can turn for all of life's healing needs.

The most important work of creating a wholistic medical system is accomplished by educating the children in the ways of natural healing. Children need to learn how their bodies work. They need to learn the reality of biological nature. The best way to teach children about the nature of earthly life is to touch them lovingly. In a healthy culture children are touched lovingly everyday.

There are many special techniques but what is really important is the intention of your Heart. If your mind is clear and your Heart full of Love your hands will heal. Massage calms and centers children the way nothing else can. If you are aware of your movement patterns you can teach your children the inner wisdom of the yogic arts.

Be aware of the balance of your movements. Move slowly and evenly. Stroke in gentle motion. Have a special place to do your massage. Your child will soon associate this place with a meditative state of mind. Everyday your child will look forward to a special rest and relaxation. S/he will experience the joys of biological regeneration. This is essential learning for knowing one's own body.

davidburns

SKIN TO SKIN

GENTLE, VERY GENTLE

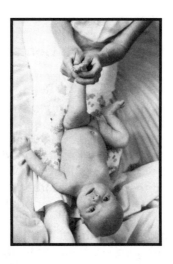

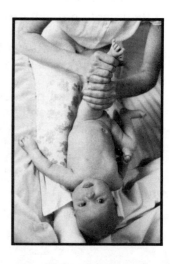

**EYE CONTACT**
**SMILE**
**GOODDAY**

SKIN    TO    SKIN

GENTLE, VERY GENTLE

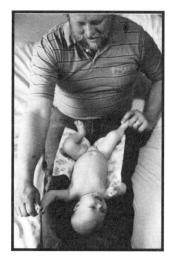

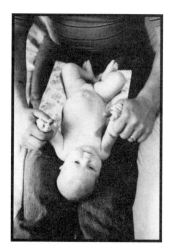

**EYE CONTACT**
**SMILE**
**GOODNIGHT**

The Children come first. This is the Way. The new people know this. This is our Testament. This is our Creed. We are not here to reclaim old words. We are here to give birth to a new world. We are the Children of Blue Corn. Our roots go all the way into the bedrock of Love.

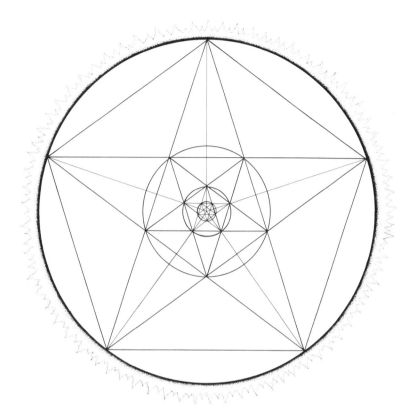

# CHAPTER FIVE

# MOTHERING AND FATHERING
## The Regeneration of Culture

All over the United States men and women are consciously conceiving, birthing, and bonding. They put their children before their careers and their family before the pursuit of money. These conscious mothers and fathers are all over the Nation. They are in the ghetto and barrio, suburb and back-hills. Such couples are found amongst all races, classes, and creeds. They all know instinctively and intuitively why they are doing what they are doing. They know that the future is in the hands of their children and that children are the center of a healthy culture. Their knowing is our best insurance that we will survive as a Nation and a People.

I asked one such couple to share their guidelines for creative parenting. I asked them to speak separately. This is their response. It pushed me to a deeper comprehension of marriage and the infinite freedom that is created when a man and woman unite. Their conscious and deliberate co-operation sanctifies their relationship.

*Dear Joshua,*

*Here are the "Guidelines." We have tried to differentiate between Mother and Father roles, but frankly, in our family, we are quite united in our approach to raising our children. In some situations Dean will tend to be strong and firm while my nature tries for a more gentle, protective understanding. And then some days I might be at my wits end with back and forth conflict, and he will come in and smooth things out. The main thing is that we support each other and create a balance so the family flows in harmonious love.*

*I hope these Guidelines satisfy your need. As parents they just seemed to flow forth, not necessarily as precepts we have mastered, but certainly as standards we aim toward. Also I would encourage parents to be patient with themselves when they don't always measure up and to avoid feelings of guilt. None of us are perfect, but we try our best.*

## GUIDELINES FOR PARENTING

Stay clear! Your children are mirrors of your moods and attitudes. You will quickly be reminded of how you are feeling by how your children are acting.

If they are freaking out, don't freak at them. It will only make things worse. Try to find out what is really bugging them.

Be consistent. Always changing your position on things will create inner turmoil and confusion. Mom and Dad should try to establish a unified program and mutually support each other.

Work at being positive. Try to build up your child's sense of the good in life. Don't look for faults or be unduly critical. Praise your children often.

Be honest in all your dealings. Children will pick up at an early age what is truth. Help them to be honest.

Be reasonable and understanding. Explain why you choose a certain path. Don't use anger as a regular practice. It is a powerful tool and used rarely will be much more effective.

Provide meaningful boundaries and restrictions. Kids will usually push to find their limits but they really appreciate knowing how far (how late, etc.) they can go.

Be flexible. You don't have to be unbending and hard nosed to keep it straight with your kids.

Accept their point of view. In fact, encourage their opinion and involve them in the decision making process of the household. Enjoy the harmony consensus can bring. Rules will be more readily obeyed if they help formulate them.

Trust your children. Believe in them. Be on their side. Let them feel your support. Let them at least start life knowing they are loved.

Don't nag. Help them develop their own sense of responsibility so the burden of their homework, clean room, the chores, and other have-to-do things is not on your shoulders. Let them hear the firmness in your voice. Once should be enough.

Develop good habits. Regularity can be healthy but of course allow for deviation from time to time.

Be available. Don't get so caught up in your own reality that you neglect your communion with your children.

Be sure to balance your love for your own children with your love for all children. They are your special ones but don't forget to be loving and fair to others.

Don't put your kids on the spot in front of other people. Try to work out your thing with them on a one to one basis unless of course a group interaction is more beneficial.

Whenever possible, help direct your children toward a creative exploration of life and toward opening up to their unique potential as human beings.

Guide, console, discipline, and above all, keep a sense of humor.

Inspire in your chidren a reverence and respect for all life. Instill in them an attitude of thanksgiving, and open them up to a loving communication with God.

Be a shining example of love for your children to follow. Don't gossip about your neighbors or play favorites. Everyone will benefit by your unconditional love.

May the Holy Spirit of Harmony
& Crystal Clear Communication
Bless your Family

**Love, Dean and Dudley Evenson**

The Evensons are creators of Soundings of the Planet in Tuscon, Arizona.

# Mothering

From the cyclic release of her egg to the filling of her breasts with colostrum, a mother surrenders to a deeply spiritual, as well as physical, process. This surrender has in some basic way made women more humane than men. Every woman is tested to her limits by mothering. Mothering is the most demanding human relationship. She is totally zeroed in by the process of procreation. Her solar plexus is extended to the core of the earth when she lets us into the flower of her Being. Her compassion is constantly tested as she protects, guides, and learns to let go.

Mothering is an art. Women who choose to stay at home are in no way inferior or less gifted than those who choose to work in other careers. In the attempt to break away from stereotypes, expectations and repressive roles, many women devalued mothering. Women who stay home with their children often have to grapple with feelings of inferiority, frustration or anger, as they try to justify, within themselves, why they are not doing "their work in the world". The fact is, mothering is VITAL work in this world. Being a mother is professional work. It is challenging work. It is creative work. The work of mothering is beneficial to mother and child and furthers the loving transformation of the world.

"Liberation" means love and responsibility. Liberation also applies to the woman who consciously chooses to remain at home with her chidren, who is true to her beliefs that her children will be most benefited by her loving guidance throughout each day. The liberated mother must liberate herself from feelings of guilt or frustration and the expectations of a society that is expecting women to be "in the work force". She challenges her second-class status in an economic system which depends upon her labor and yet disrespects her work. The liberated mother needs support: from her mate, from her circle of friends, from the community and from the nation's capital.

Good mothering needs community support. Organizations like the La Leche League, women's health clinics, women's studies departments on college and university campuses, periodicals like "Mothering" magazine, and other such sources of support and information have been a part of the process of validation essential for the work of mothering. Such support has allowed those women who bear and raise children without a male partner to manage. And they have helped those who bear children within the context of a "mate" relationship to do so with less fear of perpetuating oppressive roles.

Mothering is essential for the survival of the human race. But survival also depends upon adaptation to changing times. These days, one half of all mothers work outside the home. For most, it is due to economic necessity. For others, it is a natural extension and expression of their creativity, natural talents, and/or education. More than half of all college students today are women. More and more women long to express their education in the work force. This is as it should be. All human beings need to be creative and productive in their culture. Both men and women are needed to rebuild our nation. Such building can only be accomplished in an environment of gender equality.

It is a tremendous challenge to integrate work outside the home with the work of mothering. We have to wage a political struggle to get mothering respected in the workplace. First off, we need to get what Dana Rafael calls Furlough For Reproduction. F.F.R. is a one-year leave from work for childbirth, breastfeeding, and infant care. After this leave of absence, mother has the option to return to her position either full or part time. In addition, we must create day care centers where creative and well-paid people work with our children.

To create a culture that is beneficial for the working mother will require a total transformation of our economic system. Her fifty-nine cents (less for women of color) to his dollar is the basis of a system which routinely disregards the wellbeing of all workers. These are problems that new men and women are going to have to grapple with together. Only by working together can we create viable options for our children.

Culture naturally regenerates when mother initiates her mate into the reality of nurturance. Culture is responsive to Life. To Love. To giving. To sharing. To gentle touch. Nurturance is the basis of Life. It is the basis of everything human. If we are going to stop the fires of destruction it will be by entering into the world with the values of mother. Everything that we do must be done through her eyes. She must inform the medium of culture in which we live and grow.

## Mothering and Fathering

I recently met with a woman who had dedicated her life to healing. She was on her way to medical school, and she was determined to make progressive change within the system. While pursuing her pre-med requirements, she had taken time to learn about herbs, psychic birth control, and nutrition. She cares deeply for others. She is hungry for real knowledge. She is strong and loving. We talked about her trials dealing with scholastic preparation, tests, and colleges she wanted to get into. When the subject of children came up, she quickly said that she wasn't going to have any. I asked why, and she said there would be no time. I could sense the presence of unresolved feelings in the sound of her voice.

I shared my feelings with her. I told her that it certainly was not necessary for everyone in every lifetime to parent. But I also let her know that if she did want to have a baby, there were ways to be effective in the world and still mother—and that it is important for all kinds of women to mother. In speaking to her I realized that I was a testimony to that. My mother was a working mother, a "liberated" woman doing vital work in the world at a time when women weren't encouraged to both work and mother. Naturally, we both suffered, but have also both deeply benefited from our relationship. Both of our lives have been blessed by each other's presence in unique ways.

I asked Dr. Betty Halpern to talk about her early days as a working mother.

My mamma speaks:

*As I approach my 60th birthday, my son's request for a "statement" about my life as a working mother allows me the opportunity to reflect and examine it. My working life really began as a child in an immigrant family observing (and later aiding) in the difficult task of earning a living in a new country. Work was an expected and necessary activity—and all shared, whether in the store, housework, or baby sitting. When I entered U.C. Berkeley in 1945, work and school was the pattern. I married in 1947, graduated in January 1949, and gave birth to Joshua in March of 1949.*

*At that time, there was no support system among women. Many of my friends made dire predictions of the psychological damage I was causing by "abandoning" my children when I went to work. But none of them helped me to realize the damage I was doing to myself in not allowing my need to experience the mother-child relationship in a full, nurturing way.*

*What words of wisdom can I utter that will aid those raising children today so that the experience for the child and the adults will be mutually nourishing and satisfying? Let me make the attempt:*

## Working Mother Guidelines

*1. There needs to be a true partnership in the child-rearing so that each adult receives from and gives to the child emotional, physical and psychological pleasure. But there also needs to be time to work at both satisfying and economic tasks. This will take "ruthless" planning so that each adult gets a fair share at both important jobs: child rearing and the development and contribution of one's skills to the society.*

*2. Each adult engaged in the child-rearing needs to be constantly alert to the oppression and exploitation that takes place in society and often in the home. And just awareness of this pattern is not enough. One must put a stop to it.*

*3. There needs to be a constant reaching out to other adults and children so that the nuclear family is not an isolated, alienated, self-indulgent unit but rather one that is part of, and contributes to, the lives other adults and children in the neighborhood and community. This implies not only baby sitting, sharing of holiday celebrations and customs, sharing of materials and information—but also fighting for quality child care so that all children can have the care they deserve and all parents can more readily engage in work that is necessary and important for their economic and intellectual wellbeing.*

*4. There needs to be a real sharing of skills and competencies among the adults raising young children. No concern with "roles" here. Each person has a responsibility to contribute his/her skills and talents to the good of all in the family. We need to teach each other what we know so that each person can achieve maximum growth and development.*

*5. There needs to be real enjoyment in the process of building and raising a family. The important thing is not to suffer through this "hard" experience, but to really see and appreciate the rare beauty of people living, loving, and growing up together.*

*6. The home and family need to become the model of political and social behavior that is cooperative, respectful, validating and joyful.*

Dr. Betty Halpern

## Father: Where Is He?

Since men have not been intimately involved in the raising of children, mothering has come to be seen as "secondary" work. And yet somewhere deep inside all women is a gut level feeling that validates mothering as work. Any woman who works as a full-time mother knows this is true. If more men experienced the day-in, day-out ups and downs of full-time childcare as primary caretakers, then motherhood would be respected as the vital work that it is.

From the earliest war tribes to the anger of punk guitarists, from the creation myths of all major religions to the God of Science, there has been a stockpile of inherited confusion which the boy-child must reconcile in subtle but profoundly different ways than his sister.

Generation after generation of men have grown up and become fathers without knowing their father as a warm, fleshy, nurturing Presence. For thousands of years children have been nurtured primarily by female energy, by mother. Father instinct has been suppressed by a social structure that severs men from birth and bonding.

Both male and female feel the absence of a nurturing father. Both feel the difference between the mother who cares for them and the father who is away "providing". But the girl child remains in symbiosis with her mother for a much longer span of time. She has a ground to her identity based on what she and her mother have in common. She knows that she can one day be a mother herself. The boy child does not have a womb root. He does not spend most of his time with a same-sex parent. Even before he can control his bowels he must identify himself as "other than mother."

No matter how attentive the mother is, the male child must separate from her to discover his own gender identity. He cannot learn to relate to himself through identifying with his mother. He cannot learn to be like her without taking on the ugliest demons of this sexually-confused society. Although he spends most of his time with her, blood will never flow from his womb; he will never carry within him the Egg of Life. He cannot be protected from the world of men by his mother. And he cannot return to the world of women with her. He cannot become like her unless he commits gender suicide.

His confusion can't be mended by his mother. She was trained by her father to accept the distance between them. Even affectionate mothers touch their male children less often than they touch their female children.

However, men claim their sons early. Although they leave the actual care of the child to the mother, the son is expected to be like him. To live with her husband, the mother must treat her son differently than she treats her daughters.

A boy perceives separation from his mother as rejection. And he internalizes this feeling. The boy child is severed from his feelings, his core. To compensate, he bonds to images of masculinity associated with aggression and control. Acting strong and in control becomes a defense mechanism to hide the hurt of rejection so strongly felt in the necessary separation from mother.

For generations, men have internalized and literally incorporated these feelings of rejection. For generations men have infected their sons with stressful role models. Men have been taught to plough through stress and to repress their emotions; to strive, strain, and forget; to know themselves by Doing rather than Being. Our internal sense of being worthy of love becomes veiled by images of what it is to "be a man".

To become a man the boy must break away from his mother and begin the long process of duplicating, surpassing, and/or rebelling against the father. But with every generation, becoming a man has become more precarious. The striving and forgetting maintains the status quo but it breaks men down. No longer can they exploit their bodies the way their fathers did without inviting serious degenerative diseases at younger and younger ages. The drugs, foods, and entertainments indulged in to support their relentless striving numb and sicken them.

Beginning in the first years of life, little boys begin training for the great day when they will become men. But every step of the way is so ambiguous. The contradiction between the father's absence from the dynamics of family life and his place at the head of the table is very confusing. Somehow becoming a man has to do with his place at the head of the table. This place is not saved for the one who is doing the work of caring for the babies. It is reserved for him. Little boys are taught from the very beginning to expect the throne of the nuclear family. And yet father's absence is incorporated into the little boy's psyche. Fathers become myths — sad myths — of kings who never had princes to inherit their thrones.

## The New Man Comes Forth

A new father has emerged from the womb of Creation, just in time. He values self-knowledge more than status and God more than gold. He is a nurturing father. A Compassionate father. An entire generation of children is learning about male reality in a whole new way. When children don't have to spend their lives becoming free of the father's tyranny a tremendous burst of creative energy is liberated into the core of culture. Indeed, now, the continuation of culture depends upon the Graceful Presence of the new father.

The emergence of a new father has occurred despite the oppressive inertia of patriarchy. Few realize how difficult it is to be a father in new times. He must voluntarily transcend the false privilege which patriarchy bestows upon him. This can not be done in a monastery secluded from woman and the world. The new father learns the relativity of worldly attainments in the process of nurturing his young. By fathering he is the recipient of knowledge. By learning to be a nurturer he is enlightened. By Being Present in the infinite little moments of his child's life he is made Whole. In the process of fathering a new plexus of energy opens inside his Body.

This opening up of a new energy plexus inside the male Body has not been given status by any social or economic system. Few spiritual systems have any knowledge of such illumination. The opening enjoined by conscious male procreation is an inner reality. It can only be hinted at by metaphor. Thomas Jefferson was alluding to this inner process when he declared that revolution should occur every twenty years. He was referring to what happens when boys become men.

The impact upon a culture of men becoming fathers is life enhancing on many, many levels. There is nothing our Nation needs more than a generation of creative fathers who can teach their children how to Dance for Life. We need men who know how to manifest their creative energy into the Body politic. We need a new generation of gentle warriors. It is time for the men to stop being divided by status-rank hierarchy and start uniting through their common role as nurturers.

I asked a nurturing father to tell me how he will teach his son of male creativity. His name is Rico Baker and he practices what he preaches. He is doing it. In the Real World. With men like him we will find our way back to the good Road of Life.

Little boys do not inherit their father's throne. But they can, and do, inherit underlying attitudes from their fathers. Boys who witness their father's might and authority over their mothers must suppress their deep connection with their feminine nature. Although man has walked on the moon few men dare to let a woman into their heart.

Men have constructed gigantic civilizations to veil their basic equality with women. Every nation-state in the "civilized" world is fabricated on the basis of man's superiority. Woman's intuition and invention have been shunned by the dominant males. Men build big hospitals for the sick and pregnant; fit birthing into their busy schedules. Man's governmental policies routinely subject children to warfare. If men were bonded with their children, how could they send them off to war?

The internalized split undermines his psychological development. Although his body grows, there remains, locked within his identity, a core of confused and unresolved feelings which belong to the infant. These are the feelings which crystalize in the rage men exhibit when they lose in their relationships with women. This loss restimulates the buried reservoir of early repressed feelings locked inside the body. The original, total power which mother had over him distorts his ability to see his lover. When she exerts her autonomy, it shakes the foundation of his identity. The only way he can avoid dealing with these feelings is to "put woman in her place".

Male terror is a result of the ages-old separation of man from birth and bonding. It is instilled in children when fathers are estranged from their role as nurturer. It is passed along from father to son, but it is not coded into our genetic structure. It does not occur "because only the strongest sperm can make it up through the hostile waters of the birth canal". It does not exist because God deemed the male aggressive. Male aggression is not innate. The violence and rage of men has its origins in infancy and early childhood. It is the result of feelings of isolation and powerlessness that the male child experiences during the earliest formative stages of his identity. When, as an infant, he is shocked out of union with mother and is not provided a nurturing male to bond to, he loses touch with earth plane reality.

## What I Do That Teaches
## My Son of Creation

They say "As a seed is sown, so shall it grow." This is why your mother and I prepared ourselves in many ways before we mixed our seeds together and called for you to enter our lives. We ate the best food we could find, and, in general, only took into ourselves the kinds of experiences that would help you grow well. I was near you all along. Do you remember my voice as I massaged you and your mother while you were still inside her?

Only your sisters and I were with you and Mom as we knelt there in the warm, dimly-lit bedroom of our mountain home to watch in awe and respect your entrance into this world, coming at the rate and time just right for you. No masked stranger was there with bright lights or cold metal tools. We wanted to give you the chance to know that our lives here on Earth can begin with peace, and in trust of the total cycle of creativity. Hence, there was no cutting; things were allowed their own pace. Do you remember how, on the third day, the placenta and its cords fell off by itself, and you immediately grabbed it and held it long and gently in your little hand before letting go? Maybe this was your first creative act. We didn't cut any skin off your penis either, for we trusted that you came to us in proper form, and we especially didn't want you to enter life with the message that your beautiful little tool, the physical image of male creativity, necessarily brings with it pain. We look to your male parts as living metaphors of creation; they are not evil. And so we let you run around naked, and let your hands explore. This is also why your mother and I let you be with us in our skin and touch.

We have always kept soft cloth diapers next to your soft skin, and changed them as soon as we noticed any discomfort or wetness. Cold, wet suffering is also not to be connected with this part of your body.

Many times in your nakedness, you have shared your body's creations with us and our carpets. One of the first times I held you, that liquid sensation I have come to know and love was a true gift. This may just be the basis of artistic expression. At any rate, we have allowed you to find your own time to pee and, as you call it, "phew" in the little potty, without punishment. You are almost two years old now, and how happy we *all* feel as you carry in the potty, filled with a golden present, showing us proudly what you could do by yourself. You didn't need us to teach you (with pain) about these functions.

Inside your little sacs will grow little seeds, and someday they will even grow little tails and make ready, like pollywogs, to swim into the world. Let's plant a garden together and watch how just a few seeds make so many plants. What better way to learn of this miracle. The plants grow to feed us with beauty and nourishment. Certainly we will not want to waste them. Your little seeds can also grow into other sources of nourishment, like yourself. Do you know that you, as a child, are nourishing us with your joy and energy, and that, as you grow, you will one day come to feed us, more literally, in our old age? The soil must be prepared so that the seeds may grow strong.

We must love the earth; dirt is not filth; soil is the soul of a huge being we call the earth. It is like our mother's womb in many ways. Some people don't seem to like the earth. I think their fathers were probably gone a lot when they were little; only their mothers were around to do everything. Maybe this is also why these same people are often afraid of women and try to control them. They are little boys, grown into big boys who are afraid of their human creativity. They want to learn how to make babies in test tubes.

I sure hope I will be able to continue being with you as you grow, so that you will know that "father" is a real, available member of Creation too, not merely someone who makes night deposits and disappears in the day. You will learn that seeds are the vitally small things of fatherly creativity, like patience, gentleness, kindness, and a warm strong arm to hold little growing things.

You have known nothing but nights with our whole family in one big bed, snuggled in between warm, loving bodies, but some people put little guys like you behind bars, to sleep alone, thinking they must control them. (Certainly no child will be allowed to control *them* or interfere with their lives!) When they hear cries, they hear only manipulation. We trust that your cries are for nourishment, both for your mom's milk, and for the touch and security of soft skin. We hope you will learn from this to trust also, to let things emerge the way they ask, to believe, and to accept. So I put down my book or hammer to listen as you show me that same horse picture over and over. We think that creativity needs to follow inspirations. If you want to look at horses right now, then this is the right time to be there with your enthusiasm. This is also the reason why we are teaching your sisters right here at home, and not putting them on the bus each morning. When they want to write letters, or build a bench, *then* we do it!

Some people only learn that their fathers are for discipline. They hear, "Just wait until your father gets home! *Then* you'll be sorry!"—which is a very strange thing to be taught, isn't it? Better that we think how happy we are to see our father, and he doesn't even have to be gone!

## Mothering and Fathering

Many fathers were probably little boys whose fathers seemed to go away some place to do their creative work—at least their mothers probably said that it was more creative work than housework, so they thought they had to go away to be creative also, but look, your mom and I like it here, all of it, because we share everything—meals are fun, doing dishes is fun; it's much easier to see all of our life as creative when we are enjoying it.

Do you want to know a little secret? "Art" is a word for the special kind of creativity where beauty and truth are allowed to shine out of something we make or do. Well, a very fun way to do this is to call your *whole life* (from before birth to after death!) your art, and then you don't necessarily need to leave home to make it! Now, don't get too worried about those big concepts like "truth" and "Beauty." You are already truthful and beautiful; that's why we aren't in a big rush for you to learn our language. When you call a horse a "hoho" you speak truly, and we will also let you give your opinions on the way things are done, because we believe that truth is a matter of counsel and creative dialogue, which is not absolute. When we all put our views into the center of the circle, then we come to truth. This is why we have a family council once a week, and let everyone talk in their turn, and we all listen and appreciate your voice. This is our duty here—to speak out what we believe, even if it feels like we will seem unusual, it is best that we say our truth. In this way, children have helped many emperors to see their nakedness.

Now, I know you are inspired to do millions of things each day, so I also am helping you to do one thing at a time until finished, even if that takes two hours of looking at the same book over and over, because this is how we learn concentration. Inspiration without concentration can be like scattering our seeds again. We are aspiring to let our ideas and plans be only *suggestions*, not orders, in the hope that you and I can learn to let our creations become free agents. As you grow so quickly, I know the day of fully setting you out into the world will come very soon, and I want to teach you this "letting go" along with the "letting be" that open up the kind of space where muses and other forms of inspiration can dwell in their fullness.

This high form of art we call "our life" will also have to be let go. Those of us who are afraid of this final test will probably not risk creating smaller things, either. I pray that when this body dies, I will be blessed to continue as an example; that it will be a time also free of those masked men and other strangers and bandits, as was your birth. I pray for a time of Home Birth and Home Death, with Home School in between, so that we may best learn to accept, nurture, and let go of our creations.

As you know all too well, I make mistakes, and my fathering needs a lot more practice. I know well that the strongest teaching comes from example, and too often I do things I don't want you to learn, so I had better explain more about these also. You know those times when I get angry and yell and sometimes hurt you when you are doing perfectly O.K. things, and even beautifully creative things? Well, I sure hope that when I apologize you will believe me when I say that it's "my" problem, and not usually what you were doing. You see, I didn't have the same kind of experiences as you in many ways. My birth was in a hospital. I was taken from my mother and put in a little box. The world, from the very beginning, was a foreign place. My mother didn't give me milk from her warm breast, but from a hard bottle, and the stuff made me kind of sick (I was sick a lot as a child). I can remember waking at night in a prison-like crib. From afar came my parents' voices, but no touch. I was afraid. I was hurt for making messes; and I wasn't supposed to cry, especially as I got older. People told me I wasn't a "real man" if I cried (probably because of my parents' fears and their parents' fears and back and back and back . . .) So inside of me are these same fears and angers, and although I am coming to understand this part of myself, sometimes the fears and angers jump out. Please forgive me when these old, frightened, and angry voices take control and lead me to hurt you; believe me when I apologize. That is one of the jobs of big people—to lovingly let go of these kinds of old patterns. Sometimes we don't even realize or remember old experiences and patterns until your actions remind us, and we suddenly explode. We feel bad later and ask ourselves, "What was that all about?" and we remember (unfortunately, too late sometimes, to keep from doing things that hurt others).

You and your mother are my best teachers about these things. I want to have more patience with you. Patience is a life-long lesson. Logically, I should not get mad at you, for how can I expect you to have learned the things that I haven't learned in thirty-eight years or more? I can only continue trying to be patient with all my self-defeating stuff, so you can learn to be patient with yours, and then, the same with your son, so that this becomes the new old pattern.

As my knowledge and patience and courage and compassion grow, hopefully there will be less difference between my intent and my actions. But as you look at me out of the future, please *see my heart*. It wants to give you full potential to participate in Creation."

. . . . Christmas Day

# Mothering and Fathering

*If we are ever going to be men in Communion, we are going to have to acknowledge and forgive each other more. There is brilliance we hold back from each other. Today we can acknowledge we are God-Free, we can supplant, reinstate and deepen our "Self-Commitment" and "Self-Determinism." Some of us here have also a choice of balancing World Karma with their own chakras. They know who they are.* We must all become Noah's now. *We have this male energy to be master builders with. We are an incarnation to master the flow of our God-Self. Will we do it?*

*To balance personal and world karma with your own chakras, this is the "Ark." To bring down the healing garment for the other men and to be the example of wholeness, joy and strength (male energy) to those who are working for the "Light." To let our attitudes (chakras) be oiled by yang light (active fire) so we can* support and sponsor other men in becoming leaders and builders of the new man *and the new world.*

Bhakta

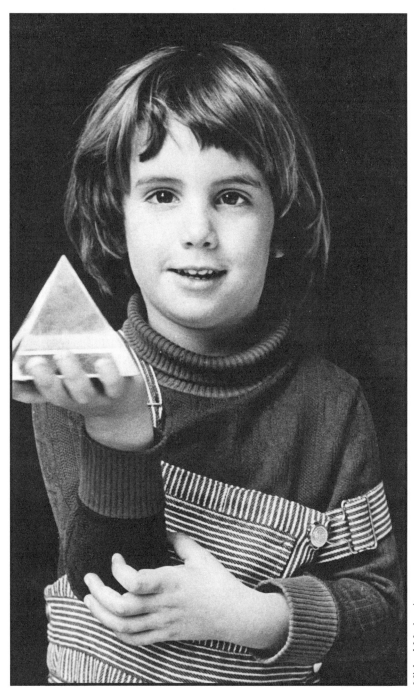

Michael Markowitz

The following story is also about a man's journey into fatherhood. But it is a different path. This is the story of an awakening which occurred against great odds. But awaken he did and to this day he continues to nurture his beautiful daughter.

## Part One: The Stage is Set.

You could say I was an atheist when it came to the subject of children. My generation is the generation of the proclaimed, acclaimed, mystified, rarified, indulgent, desirous self. The self that so easily identifies with the All, but often times limits its boundaries to any one person, place, or experience. Thus is born the so-called artist, mystic, seeker, potential sage, the detached Krishna playing with the sweet young gopis. A veritable merry-go-round of adventure. Wheeeeeee!

But what of children? Children? you ask: those dependent, weak, needy, wailing, failing illusions of time, the product of sex, of ego, of the repulsive chain of incarnation. No, no, a thousand times no! My freedom, my God, my guru, my karma, my genitals, my art, my, my, my. And so it went until the fateful moment, entwined in passionate interplay, when sperm met egg, overriding the all-prevailing concepts of the intellectual mind.

## Part Two: Continuation of Denial. Holding Out.

1. Ahh! The pleasure of sex, orgasm. Such delightful fun. Of course we agree that it's purely recreational, healing vibrations, you know—good for the body, mind, and soul, etc. . . . don't worry, I'll hold my semen. Ahhhhh . . . oops.

2. Pregnant? . . . you're joking! No way . . . the curse! My freedom. Abortion is the only resolution. Here's the money. Please get rid of it. That was close. This sex thing is getting out of hand. I must read Gandhi one more time.

3. What? Can't be done? O.K., panic, if you keep the baby I'm totally out of the picture. Goodbye. Oh, God . . . my karma . . . . !!!

So all during the pregnancy I withdrew my support: emotionally, economically, and much of the time even as a friend. If there was ever a time I was clear about the relationship, this was it. She had so agreed that if I wished to remain out of the picture of this being's arrival, coming-out party and eventual caretaking, so be it and she would handle the consequences and responsibility. I should have received the "schmuck of the year" award for the role I played during the pregnancy.

So I kept aloof, choosing to remain in my ambivalent joy of detached pessimism, little realizing that subconsciously I was being prepared for a much greater role as father.

## Part Three: Realization

I was living on the island of Maui at the time of my baby's birth in California. I was very involved in my escapades, as usual, and only occasionally would I allow Mama and Baby to enter my mind.

But then one day, actually quite suddenly, I began to really wonder about this newborn being that, through my seed, came to be. I thereby decided to complete my experience on Maui, travel to California, and meet this baby who had just arrived. It took six weeks from the time of the birth to complete my destiny on Mother Maui. As I look back, I realize that missing my daughter's birth was my reward for my unsupportive attitude.

## Part Four: Enlightenment—Arrival

I'll never forget the *moment* I saw my daughter for the first time. I wasn't prepared for the enlightenment she suddenly brought on. My entire being for three thousand years back flashed before my very eyes. Encapsulated within her tiny form was an entire history of my people and it brought upon me such a rush of love, a recognition of the innocent, surrendered self—so beautiful, so intimately connected—that I've never been the same since. That little miracle did more for my awareness in fifteen seconds than fourteen years of reading books on awareness had. Truly, it has been one of the greatest threshold experiences of my adult life and I believe it will continue to be so throughout the remainder of my time on Earth.

So, fellow travelers of time, the burden of children is only another concept caught within the intellectual mind. Free yourself forever of all binding concepts thereof and witness the love that emerges as God, the Father-Mother-Child.

**Love, Richard Koobatian**

*Richard is a sculptor.*

## Healing the Father Within

All men who never received the loving grace of their fathers have the tremendous task of reconciling with the father that lives in their psyche. It does no good to simply deny him as he seemed to deny us. We barter off too cheaply what is noble in him if we do. And besides, there is no escape from our fathers. We are still like him though we may take a new name, wear long hair, or go gay. Our father will still be sitting at the head of our table, incorporated into our psyches. In order to reconcile with Father, we must understand how we—and our sons—become men/fathers. It is up to us to begin to comprehend some of the intricate dynamics of male gender identity. We need to comprehend what the male child experiences and what he models himself after.

My most vivid memory of my boyhood days with my father is of the two of us alone in our dimly-lit living room. I was seven years old. Leadbelly, the great, soulful folksinger, was singing "Goodnight Irene" on the phonograph. My father's sister was named Irene, and as long as I had known of her, she had been in the hospital. My father began to cry. He cried right where I could see him. I remember being stunned. I only wish he had called me to him and let me feel his tears on my cheek.

Like many fathers and sons of that time, we had a great distance between us. The separation between us was not of our own making. It was created before either of us arrived on this sweet earth. It was the result of generations of broken bonds between fathers and sons. Like many boys, I had no conscious awareness of the separation. I lived in a zone between my imagination and the needs of my body.

Some old report cards, which I found buried away in the basement, helped remind me of how the adult world perceived me.

*"I feel that Joshua is strongly motivated to function as a mature adult, rather than as a child with the right to experience appropriately immature stages of development. I wish he could get the same satisfaction from being the sensitive nine-year-old that he is as he does turning his precocity towards aping adult sophistication."*

*"Joshua is learning to come to grips with his problems. He is less tense, and is gaining in confidence. He needs a lot of praise and encouragement. He feels under pressure, much of it self-imposed . . ."*

*"Joshua needs to gain emotional stability. His highs are too intense, and his lows too frustrating. But he really makes words work for him in his stories. Today he wrote 'the equator is invisible.' But behavior-wise, his defiant carelessness has acted up again."*

Indeed I was hunting for something "invisible." I only wish I could have screamed out poems of need from the jungle-gyms of my gradeschool playgrounds. I only wish I had been asked what I was really feeling. I would have called out for my father. For closeness with a Man Who Loves Me.

I don't have to call out secretly anymore. After many years of struggle and hard work, my father is my best friend. I trust his counsel. Each year we accept each other more. We dream of each other. He's had psychic dreams intuiting what I was going through before I told him (or anyone else). Our Solar Plexus center has unified.

In the mid-sixties, my father opened up to Spirit. He worked with Fritz Perls at the Esalen Institute, and then went on to experience primal therapy. When he came out of his intensive, he was deeply open to me in ways he had never been before. He had cleared out his own father's ghost.

# Mothering and Fathering

*It took me thirty years after my father's death to realize that my enduring "anger" at him was caused by my feeling that he had never blessed me—so that once I experienced the damnable hurt of feeling unblessed, my love for him came through and we have been close ever since.*

Reuben Halpern
*Live Your Health*

Since those days my father has blessed me freely. He has let his love for me be openly expressed. His openness is a major catalyst of my life.

It was during a break-through experience while traveling with my father in the desert that *Children* was first envisioned. We were finishing a two-year collaboration on *Live Your Health.* Little did we know that the bookmaking process was going to initiate healing. Traveling together was very intense. We had never really been together day in and day out. We began to hassle. Little fights. Big fights. Finally one morning while walking, my father turned to me and said, "Look, I've noticed a lot of our hassles are old stuff. Let's be clear about what is going on in the here and now and what is carried over."

Then, that night, after he had gone upstairs to sleep, I watched a movie on T.V. about a long-distance runner in prison. Something about the prison scenes and all the locked-up men and that day's experience with my father caused an opening in me. I began to cry. I remembered. I cried for my father and for his love and I cried for all the fathers who wanted to love their sons but did not know how. The next morning I began a journal out of which this book was born.

Now, my father and I cry together. He is one of the few people that I feel safe weeping with. We have dared to remember. We both call out to each other now. The healing process continues. We know that the legacy of father/son separation cannot be wiped out immediately. But we have stuck to our vision. Slowly and consistently we have begun to decipher the confusing messages keeping us apart. We are beginning to nurture each other.

Healing is possible between all fathers and sons. If my dad and I could do it, all can. All it takes is consistent focus and clarity of intention. As a man I knew that I had to enter into an abiding communion with my father. I knew that before I died I needed to be at peace with the sun. With the Male force of nature. With the pulsating Body of poetry in motion. I set my mind on discovering the reality of the Bond.

In many ways the healing is easier for me than him because his father is dead. My father is still alive and so can be in ways totally spontaneous. Indeed, that is the best way to approach father. Out of nowhere shower him with love. Love works wonders. Listen to this poem my father wrote for me.

*I*
*Do you remember*
*the cup I gave you?*
*You kept it a long time*
*Though I saw it but once since*
*Dimly shining in your closet.*
*I think you lost it*
*Or abandoned it*
*Somewhere*
*Maybe where I last saw mine*
*I know you want to look with me*
*For both*
*But what if mine*
*(If it still exists)*
*Crumbles*
*Just with a touch?*

*II*
*I hate words now*
*But don't you see*
*That without them or with them*
*I could be naked*
*Or have you always known that*
*And not cared?—but then you*
*Would have loved me*
*All these closeted years*
*Maybe I feared that most*

*III*
*If we look*
*Let's use as few words as possible*

Our love is tough. The bond is spiritual. Though I may not see my father for months on end he is present. And his presence supports my liberation. It's going to be very hard to carry on without him. I take refuge knowing we will be drawn together again. I am looking forward to the next round with my father.

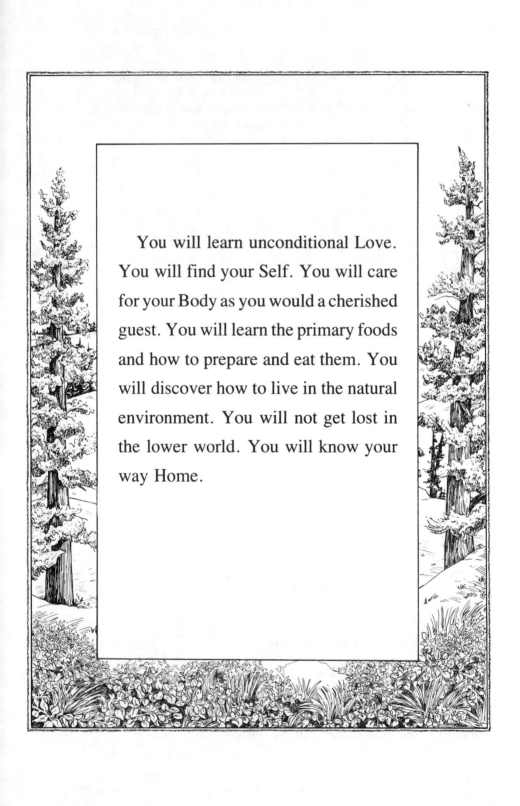

You will learn unconditional Love. You will find your Self. You will care for your Body as you would a cherished guest. You will learn the primary foods and how to prepare and eat them. You will discover how to live in the natural environment. You will not get lost in the lower world. You will know your way Home.

# CHAPTER SIX

# LEARNING SELF-RELIANCE
## Establishing the Basis

The psyche forms while in a cocoon of protection. For nine months in the blisswaters we attune to Her. When we emerge we cling to Her. She gives us security, tranquility, and bliss. She is everything. We are connected to her body and mind. We breathe in her shadow. From the very beginning both male and female children absorb the Essence of Mother into the core of their psyche. In the first months and years of life the subconscious themes of the anima are scripted out on the synapses of the nervous system. Awareness of Father is gradual. We begin to notice him while suckling. From her arms we approach Him. She is the gateway, the eye of the needle. By the time a child is three s/he has integrated the Essence of mother/father into the core of his/her Being. The first three years are a progression from mother to father to Self.

Children are the center of a healthy culture. Community life revolves around the tender needs of the babes. The parents design and build a world where their children may dance in peace. They protect their children from evil. The first three years of every incarnation are dependent upon nurturance and protection. The human baby is the most helpless creature on earth.

# Weaning

In a healthy culture there is natural and harmonious transition from the blisswaters of the womb to the sweet milk of the breast; from milk to solid food; from mother to father. In order for this transition to be harmonious and for the child to willingly give up the breast, he/she must receive the wholesome foods of the earth. Only whole foods offer the variety of flavors, textures, and nutrition the child needs. When a child is forced to exchange his/her natural appetite for superficial tastes, crucial learning processes are impaired. Chewing teaches and requires the ability to focus. To chew, one must focus. But to chew properly, there must be wholesome food to chew on. If food is too sweet, salty, spicy, the child sucks and gulps, but does not learn to masticate.

Suckling is relatively easy compared to weaning. The mother must know when to stop giving the nipple. Nursing for too long restricts the child's freedom. She must also know when her need for regeneration must take precedence over her child's need for milk. This is especially crucial if another child is in the ethers. Proper spacing of children allows for a period of time to recycle nourishment, build up reserves, and bleed. Indeed, proper weaning is as important to the development of Self reliance as is breastfeeding. In a healthy culture this transition is facilitated by father. Father is an extension of mother's breast. The function father fulfills in weaning is as important to the development of the child as is the sweet milk. When father is there with good food in hand, mother is spared the brunt of the weaning child's anger. Indeed, anger is not inherent in weaning. It is possible to graduate from sweet milk to good food without any fuss. It is possible to gratefully give up the erect nipple for the fruit, greens and grain of this sweet earth. The transition from absolute dependence upon mother is easy if a daily routine is established which includes father in the care of the Body.

Truly, the Tree of Life is coming back to Life. The new father is here. He is in tune with the earth and the processes of maturation. Listen to these father-weaning stories and be gladdened by the Presence of male creativity.

# Father Weaning Story No. 1

We began a night-weaning with Jamil in which I, his father, sat up with him for four nights and rocked him in the rocking chair, then slept with him when he finally went to sleep. But with time and changes (and traveling), he went back to nursing at night. Finally, at seventeen months, he was nursing a lot, and had become whiney and clinging with his mother, who needed a break.

He'd been very good and happy with me, so we decided that I'd take him to Santa Cruz, visit old friends, and do the big weaning. The following is a journal of those days.

### Tuesday, First Day

Packed up the VW van and headed out. Jamil was happy all the way and went to sleep (thank God!) 'til I got over the Golden Gate Bridge. I stopped at a little pull-off in the road where there were some far-out twisted trees. Jamil had some homemade goat's milk yogurt and apple-sauce. He put my new straw hat on and peeked through the holes and laughed and said, "Boo!" after me.

He stayed happy until maybe Los Altos, when I stopped and fed him again. We made it to Los Gatos where we stopped at a huge park with a very fancy children's playground. Then we drove straight on to Santa Cruz, though the Med-Fly inspection, to friend Lizzy's for a warm-hearted reception. Being out of the car, Jamil was again perfectly happy seeing all the beautiful children and animals there.

We went out to eat and on the way we ran into another friend who needed to take care of an old woman that night. She wanted someone to watch her little four-year-old boy. So, I slept there in the van with Jamil. Jamil went to sleep easily, but about 4:30 a.m. he started to cry. I roused myself, got dressed and took him into the house. After a little walk, he was perfectly happy and babbling away. I gave him some grapes and made applesauce and rice. He only ate some of the grapes and in about an hour we both went back to sleep.

I got up at 8:10 and went into the house. The four-year-old was sitting up, all dressed, with a hard hat on, playing with his toys. I gave him some applesauce and at 8:30 his mother came home. Jamil got up maybe an hour later, came in and ate well. Then I went out to sell some beeswax candles with him and to visit some friends. I took him to the big park in town and then, after some shopping, back to where we were staying.

## Learning Self-Reliance

He had been happy all day. He had rice and avocado for lunch. He ate a couple of bananas, too. His appetite was very strong, but easily satisfied. I gave him a shower and he played with all of Lizzy's stuff.

That night (Wednesday), Jamil went easily to sleep and slept until 4:40. Then I got up, took him into the house, changed his diaper and gave him some more of the sour grapes that he liked. After about 45 minutes, he got sleepy again and took a nap. We went through the day very smoothly.

### Thursday Night

Jamil was teething, cutting a molar. He cried for a while before he went to sleep, but began to understand about teeth. He worked it out on his own and then came to me and went to sleep. He woke up about 5:30 a.m., but went back to sleep until about 7:00. Then we got up, had a breakfast of rice and vegetables, and went out for the day. He wasn't eating the applesauce, the goat milk or the yogurt that I bought for him.

We went through a couple more nights of teething; then that molar came through! He slept until about 7:00 in the morning and seemed to be very happy. He ate a lot and was very fond of avocados, which he called "go-gah-cah."

Sunday morning was a little trying, going to the crowded flea market and then food shopping. Then I went to the park to play volleyball, but that wasn't much fun either. Did shiatsu on a friend that night and she was able to get rid of her headache. Jamil was already asleep, but woke up crying and I went and put him to sleep. We slept good that night and in the morning we got up, got our things together and said our good-byes. We got some food at Staff of Life and went up to Molly and Nathan's.

There was a fire in the fireplace and good conversation. Napoleon, the dog, who is half Pit Bull and half I-don't-know-what, was lying on a pillow by the fire. Jamil slipped away to the kitchen and came back with a handful of dog food, which he fed to Napoleon. Then we left for Sonoma.

Jamil fell right asleep right away and slept until we neared Pacifica. We stopped and had some food overlooking the bay and San Francisco. We drove on happily and Jamil fell asleep again after a while, just until we made it to the Cotati co-op. I got him some carrot juice and "go-gah-cah." He sat naked in the car seat, ate and made a mess of it. But it was easily cleaned and we made it all the way home.

His mother was there to greet us. Jamil acted distant at first, but soon warmed up. *And,* he wasn't into the breast! He pointed to them a few times, but never made a fuss and seemed perfectly content.

**Love, John**

John is an acupuncturist.

# Father Weaning Story No. 2

### Adam's Adventure

The time comes into every life when the attachments that we cling to must fall away. Our human condition is constantly changing. The bonds between Mother and child are very strong. Nursing feeds the child on all levels: physical, emotional, spiritual. As the child grows, these needs can be fulfilled in other ways.

Weaning is inevitable and the timing depends on the individual needs of Mother and child. My wife was feeling a bit drained of energy and very tired. So when my son was twenty-two months old, we decided it was time for his weaning. And what better way to accomplish it than to make it an adventure. My wife and I had been sharing our childcare as equally as possible and, since we work from home, I had already developed a strong trusting relationship with my son. So when my best friend came through California on his way to Arizona, we were ready. We subtly prepared our child by telling him of the great adventure he was about to have, a journey to the desert and the mountains to experience his first taste of independence.

He seemed willing enough but when the moment finally came to leave, he was not too happy. Off we went, and I began to learn what it must be like to be a mother — the patience, the compassion and the surrender to the child's needs. We were on the road for three days, Adam hardly moving from my lap at all. My back began to hurt from not being able to stretch or move. There were other friends that Adam liked, but I was his rock — his only comfort. His happiness and exuberance and the security of mother and home had vanished.

For many days he was silent. No smiles, no squeals, not even tears; he was in a trance-like state, wondering, I suppose, what this new world would be like. His emotions must have been turbulent. He wasn't even hungry. The most I could get him to eat were a few oranges and apples. My friends tried to cheer him up and get him to laugh, but it was many days before they were successful. After about four or five days of travel, we arrived at a friend's house in Arizona. There were children there, but Adam wasn't interested. The only person he knew and could trust was his dad. There was a mom there who looked trustworthy and she succeeded in getting him to eat some solid food. The veil was slowly lifting.

Another purpose of our trip was to make music and do some recording. But Adam's needs came first, and he didn't appreciate my attempts at having some space so mostly we played music while he was sleeping. Adam still was not happy, even with a child's playroom and lots of toys.

So now it was time to go to the mountain to visit our close friends who have a baby the same age as Adam. This was my ace in the hole. We had lived with them the year before and Adam remembered his friend Elijah.

There's something magical about the mountains, I could see Adam getting more excited. The mountains were white and very peaceful and after traversing the roads, we reached the warm mountain cabin and our friends. Adam was more at ease now and slowly getting used to his new independence. Although he needed attention all day long, we managed to get some work done at night. Adam's appetite returned and he began to eat a lot of food. After three days, our music sessions were done. We went off to the desert to celebrate before returning home. Adam was really enjoying traveling now, looking out the windows at everything there was to see. It was great to see him happy and smiling.

We all soaked in the hot springs for a couple of days and now we were two weeks away and it was time to return. Adam was really excited about flying, and he behaved like a perfect gentleman, as long as there was enough food around. After two to three hours in the air we touched down and there, waiting patiently at the gate, was Adam's mother.

He was mildly interested in nursing when he got home, but his mom explained to him that the milk was gone and he was old enought to eat. So, Adam came home weaned and happy.

Love, Aziz

Aziz is a musician.

## Father Weaning Story No. 3

### Caymin's Weaning

We first night-weaned Caymin when she was not much over a year because Diane was working at night, so I had to put Caymin to sleep. As people had led us to expect, this took about three nights. We all went to sleep as usual, but Diane did not nurse Caymin to sleep or during the night when she roused (though she did nurse after light in the mornings). This night weaning gave me a lot more freedom: instead of having to pace the floor or walk the street for hours every night, I eventually was able to put Caymin to bed and have her go to sleep easily, even allowing me to leave the room as she fell asleep.

We later resumed nursing at night, but after that, when Diane entered midwifery school, I night-weaned Caymin again. This time, due to Diane's erratic schedule, Caymin often did not get to nurse for whole days. This seemed to cause more discomfort to Diane because of full breasts than to Caymin. I'd sometimes have to drive Caymin to the clinic to relieve them both.

At last, when Caymin was 20 months old, all three of us went for a visit to my parents, but Diane had to return after only one day. Caymin and I stayed on for five more days, and that was her weaning. She got plenty of attention and plenty of food during the visit, and was happy the whole time, charming her grandparents totally. Diane and I had worried that she might not be in such a good mood due to her not nursing, and also had not decided whether to resume nursing when we returned.

Diane felt that she'd like to nurse only occasionally, once or twice a day, but neither of us expected this to be possible. Caymin had, maybe due to Diane's schedule, reached a point before our visit to the grandparents where she would seldom let Diane alone, wanting to nurse every few minutes. She was fine, though, when Diane wasn't around. Diane was looking for a more balanced relationship with her daughter.

So Caymin and I returned from the visit to find not only absolutely no indication from Caymin of wanting to nurse, but a more happy child in every way. To this day, two months later, Caymin occasionally plays with the tits and laughs, even playfully sucking for a moment, but seems happily weaned as she approaches the age of two.

## From a Single-Father

*Dear Joshua,*

*At first I was very impatient with the whole feeding scene. But after a few days I realized that my attitude was affecting my babe so I cooled it and just relaxed into meal times. Of course, I never thought that I would be doing all this, but there's a lot of things I never thought I'd be doing. Anyway, I had to do it. Due to circumstances I'd rather not go into here, I was a single father, and I really didn't know what to do. However, I discovered that if I just paid attention to what was happening and really listened for the signals, it'd work out.*

*Taking care of Michelle has taught me the importance of eating well. When I feed her stuff that is not so great, she gets stuffy-nosed and cranky. When I feed her balanced nutritious meals, she is mellow and feisty.*

*I really flashed on your questions because you asked about the happy kitchen. That's really important. I do not go into the kitchen if I'm uptight. If she's hungry and I am uptight, I try the best that I can to clear it through yoga or other means, and then feed. If she's really hungry, I just start saying a mantra like "yum yum, chew chew, the food is good and so are you" or something silly, just to liven it up a little. I agree with you, Joshua, a happy kitchen is really where it's at. And it's hard. So much of the drudgery of householding gets centered on the kitchen. I am trying in my humble way to do what I can. It's my love for Michelle that makes it possible. God bless you, Brother of Light, may your words be heard all over the world.*

*— Michael*

Proper weaning teaches the child how to inhabit their own body. Weaning is not just a matter of giving up the tit. It is a process of learning how to be an independent being. During weaning the child becomes ready for an enormous range of new impressions. The most rapid learning years of brain development occur during weaning. As the child comes off the breast a new world must be mastered. The matrix of life gradually shifts from mother to father. Thus the child learns that both genders can be nurturing forces. This learning changes everything.

## Beginning Solids

When it is time for baby to begin solid foods, it is best to prepare whatever is to be fed, which means to shun canned or bottled baby foods and stay out of commercial supermarkets. My investigations, (in 1971) which led to congressional hearings regarding baby food, showed that baby food manufacturers, like companies and businesses everywhere, are primarily motivated by profit. Salt, M.S.G., and modified food starch are all added to the grossly over-cooked baby food material. M.S.G. gives tang back to the devitaliz-ed food (unfortunately, it also causes cancer in the bladders of mice). The salt is for Mama and Papa's taste (and it begins the development of a salt habit, in preparation for future years of hypertension). The modified food starch holds it all together (although many healers feel that children should not be given any starch in the first year of life, least of all refined starch, because babies do not have the proper teeth to chew and digest this substance.)

Your little one needs vital food to optimally mature. Staying out of commercial markets may seem difficult, but it is worth the ef-fort. Naturally grown food does not contain harmful substances and chemicals. A child is delicate and tender. The less irritation, the happier s/he will be. The better the start, the stronger s/he will be able to meet the world. Natural food stores, neighborhood food groups, gardens, local farmers, wild food, and abandoned orchards offer many opportunities for creative food gathering.

This article is by Peggy O'Mara McMahon, founder of Mothering Magazine.

When solids are introduced, the weaning process begins.

Breastmilk is the superior food. Solids are the supplement. When you are beginning solids, remember to nurse first so that your milk supply is not affected.

Solids are begun because the natural supply of iron in the baby's body from birth begins to be depleted. While it is generally recommend-ed that solids be introduced during the middle of the first year of life, there is evidence that iron reaches the baby through the breast-milk beyond the sixth month. Gradually introducing solids between six to nine months has worked for many mothers.

Begin introducing solids slowly. Do not expect three meals a day at once.

Expect back-sliding. There will still be days when he will eat nothing and want to nurse seemingly all day, especially if he is sick or feeling bad or teething or making big strides in physical or verbal development.

Begin with one food at a time. As you add new foods, give him just one new food at a time for a few days in order to determine if he is sensitive to any new foods.

The development of teeth is an indication that the body has begun to develop the necessary enzymes for food digestion.

Many foods are easier to digest than others. Some foods are allergenic in nature and should be delayed until your child's digestive system is more developed. A child, for example, who was sensitive to dairy products through your breastmilk, may be able to tolerate a drink of milk after he is a year old. A baby who gets a rash from orange juice may be able to enjoy it when he is two.

Some common allergenic foods are cow's milk (dairy products), citrus (especially orange juice), nuts, tomatoes, chocolate, strawberries, corn, wheat, fish. It may be better to wait until after your child is one year old to introduce these foods, especially in families with allergy histories.

Fruits are a good food group to begin with (except for citrus and berries, as they can be allergenic). Begin with one fruit at a time, preferably those in season. Then try vegetables, cereals, grains. Some fruits can be mashed raw, scraped or grated. Other fruits and vegetables can be steamed and ground up in a baby food grinder or a blender. Bananas, apples, pears, peaches, carrots, potatoes and other naturally soft foods are good beginning foods. Make your new food choices based on what you know about that food. Is it hard to digest? Are some people allergic to it? How close to its natural state will it be when eaten by your child? (Meat, for example, is often given to children early and usually does not cause any allergic reactions, but as it must be cooked, ground and tampered with quite a bit to make it soft enough for a child, it may be a food to postpone until closer to the first year of life. Likewise, tofu is a bean product and beans are harder to digest than other foods so some caution should be used here too.)

Your child won't use a spoon well until he's a year or so, but he will enjoy finger foods and eating with his fingers up to that time. Some children will not want to be fed and will only like finger foods until they can feed themselves. Expect messes and much "creative" tactile exploration. Finger foods include carrot sticks (lightly steamed or raw), peas, fruit slices, anything which can be gummed by the toothless.

Some foods are appealing in one form but not in another. Raw carrots may be preferred over cooked carrots. Preferences may change without notice.

Body contact is important in the process of introducing solids. Sit your baby on your lap and give him tastes with your fingers. When he is comfortable in a high-chair and is eating several different foods, you can put two or three varieties in a muffin tin and let him make his own choices.

When your child reaches the four month grabbing stage, he will show interest in what you are eating in an effort to understand the world orally (his most developed sense is taste). This does not mean he is ready for solids, but only interested in putting everything in his mouth. Signs that he is ready for solids are elusive and indefinite. He may be fussy, want to nurse all the time for days and have already gotten his first teeth. Generally, however, there is an increased sense of anxiety for the mother who wonders, "Is it time?" If he's close to six months and you feel this anxiety, give him a little something and see what happens.

Regular eating habits, sit-down meals, three times a day at about the same time each day, help to establish good eating routines.

Encourage your child by commenting on eating and ignoring not eating. Trust that your child can judge when he is hungry and how much to eat if you provide him with wholesome, well-balanced foods in as natural a state as possible. Don't however, let your child wait too long in hunger or the hunger will pass and he will not eat as well as he might have.

If you're feeling rushed, postpone eating during the early months for a bit until you are more relaxed. Enjoy mealtimes and your child will too.

Peggy O'Mara McMahon

■　　■　　■

## Potty-Training

Teaching children how to live in the body is more essential to the health of a culture than the running of computers, trucks and armies. The one who changes the soiled diapers teaches the child the complex inter-relationship between matter and spirit. It is important to teach the children the nature of earthly existence.

Nature is a circle dance. We are tubular transmutators of Divine Energy. What goes in the mouth corresponds to what comes out the anus. Teach your children of the Unity. Feed them wisely and let them find their own rhythm. Go slow. Don't hurry them.

One of the most impressionable experiences children have is their diapering and potty training. The care-giver must validate the baby's body while removing the soiled diaper. Gently wash and wipe. Gently dry, powder and oil the delicate flesh. Teach the baby first hand that life is compassionate. This has a profound impact upon the psyche, and all subsequent interrelationships. All relationships involve trust and surrender. As Dorothy Dinnerstein lucidly points out in her book *"The Mermaid and the Minotaur,"* the rough handling of the infant during diaper changing sets the stage for all subsequent tyrannies of life.

Parents can take out their feelings of resentment concerning parenthood while diaper-changing. If you have a difficult time relating to this observation, try this simple exercise: get naked and put yourself in the position of a child having his/her diapers changed. The residues of invalidation seem to cling to the backs of the thighs of humans of both sexes. This is where women often cover themselves in fat. This is where men cut themselves off.

Our societal associations with this invalidation are expressed in the use of disposable diapers. The same media which sell our children sugar-coated ding-dongs for breakfast would like us to swaddle our young in chemically-treated fecal-disposers. These ugly plastic packages hold feces nice and clean. They are even perfumed so that no one has to smell baby's excrement. (Yet, smelling baby's excrement is an essential way for parents to be in touch with the health of their child.) It has been proven that perfume can cause skin disorders and interfere with the baby's natural ability to smell. The use of disposable diapers is part and parcel of society's alienation from nature and the earth. Wrapping the genitals in plastic is symbolic of our sexual confusion.

One of the most important lessons of early life is how to shit. Teach your children how to squat. Do not condition them to the Babylonic throne called toilet. The modern toilet is not conducive to health. Nor is it conducive to ecological well being. If possible adapt your toilet so that it can be squatted on. Let's begin to respect the innate workings of the Body so that our young may learn to defend their instincts from a world that has lost all semblance of its connection to nature.

# WE REMEMBER

We remember each birth
we write a song for each one
we say a prayer for each one

we remember each baby
will some day be hungry
and that the real hunger of life is for love
we remember each birth

for he/she will die
and there will be no more body
awakening each day to greet the sun

Lorienne Brightsong

Learning Self-Reliance

## Forming Play Groups

On this earth, in this body, spinning around the sun, we all begin in our mother's womb and emerge from the blisswaters with a tremendous need for Love. She is our first teacher. From her solar plexus, Life is sustained in us; from her Being comes our food; in the radiance of her protection we are given safety to grow. Through her we are introduced to our earthly father. The initial ground of Being is between mother and father. We are all the apex of a psychological triangle whose base is mother/father.

But though we depend upon them (absolutely) to bring us in, we do not belong to them. As Kahlil Gibran in *The Prophet* said, "Your children are not your children. They are the sons and daughters of life's longing for itself. They come through you but not from you. And though they are with you yet they belong not to you." Each human being is a unique "I". Children have a deep and constant need to experience the world through their own eyes. Parents cannot provide for all the needs of their children. The best of homes is a stifling place when the door to the world does not open.

One of the most crucial learning experiences of early life is successfully venturing forth from the safety of the family and exploring the world. Opening the family door is the culmination of crawling, walking, and learning to speak. Children need to explore the wider world. They need to explore from the safety of the home to forge a healthy lifeline away from mother/father. It is upon this lifeline that a viable sense of independence is created.

Children need a protective radiance to courageously venture forth. This aura of protection is spiritual. I have lived with Gypsy mothers in their encampments where the quality of protection was more supportive than in the wealthiest suburbs. Love is a quality which no economic system or government can control.

One of the most precious scenes I have ever witnessed was a child taking his first big steps. I was living in a trailer park on the outskirts of town. Many of the families didn't even have trailers. They had tents. Some were migrant workers, some were families on the move. I got to be friends with a young single mom. She lived in a tent with her two children. They were very poor, but she made their space feel orderly and safe. One night we were sitting around the fire cooking some dinner when her little boy Gabriel came up and asked her for the flashlight so he could go visit his buddy across the way. She handed it to him and told him to be careful and come home soon. He was off. When he returned, he was a changed little boy. He had crossed over a threshold. His three-year-old eyes shone with a victory that would long bolster him in all of his subsequent explorations. (He's now earning A's in a college prep-school.)

All children experience such explorations in their own way. Everyone takes their first hesitant steps with a unique gait and sway. We all learn to walk and we all long to explore. For most of us, the first consistent explorations are involved with play groups, pre-schools, and other such organized learning experiences. These are our first daily lessons in what the wider world is like. These first experiences are crucial for integration into community. The seemingly simple exercise of playing with others lays the foundation for how we will play throughout our entire school life. Processes occur within us while in the company of other children which both guide and force us into our place in the group.


As our children grow they are socialized, whether consciously or unconsciously. Parents and all those who know children to be the builders of tomorrow are challenged to initiate processes of social organization which promote health, self-esteem, and cooperation. This learning begins at home but must, eventually, reach beyond the home so that alliances can be formed within the larger community.

The development of play groups and pre-schools which are designed to be conducive to the growth of our children's loving potential is an essential requirement for social transformation. Every child deserves friends. The pre-school experience sets patterns for social involvement and learning which enrich the child's knowledge for an entire lifetime. It takes careful planning and great skill to create an environment that is truly conducive to positive socialization.

Play is not just random hilarity. It is a continuous "level of groove" that is spontaneous in well-balanced joyfulness. Play is the essence of learning. When our first educational experiences feel like play, all of life's lessons can be received with a quality of openness. When children tackle new learning in a playful way, their capacity for success is enhanced. The instinct to play is one which pre-dates language. Children want to play with other children, and give and receive love. Young human beings surge with life's most precious energy. They delight in sharing with others.

Learning Self-Reliance

The age at which most children begin pre-school coincides with the first use of language. This is really quite natural. Words are our principal tools of communication. Mental processes are built through the medium of these sounds that hold meaning. Identity is shaped by voice.

Young children hear and feel the power of words. They want to talk. They need to learn language to comprehend life. A play group or pre-school experience gives a child an opportunity to communicate in a cooperative setting.

Play groups and pre-schools give children an expanded awareness of the world. As they experience their first serious interaction with peers, they also see role models in other mothers and fathers. The newly forming minds of the young develop optimally when in contact with harmonious and happy people. Children have a tremendous need to learn first-hand. In developing play groups and pre-schools, parents are challenged to design an environment conducive to play as well as to provide positive, wholesome role models.

Play groups provide parents space to dialogue on the subject of child-raising — as well as on the quality of their own lives. As a cohesive unit, parents are challenged to formulate policies that affect both their own and other children's health. Inevitably, nutrition comes up for review. See to it that their first communal food is served with grace. Utilize the play group community as a network of support.

## Simple, Complete Meals for the Play Group

It is time to raise a generation of children who know from whence they come. Who are One with the earth. Who are proud to be earthlings. Who know the earth and sun as Mother and Father. One of the most important lessons of life is knowing how to feed oneself. Teach your children where food comes from. Grow your own. And give support to your local farmers. Wherever you are you can establish a healthy nutritional pattern for your family.

Growing good food can be done anywhere — even in a tiny city apartment. Jars full of growing sprouts convert any kitchen or small space into an all-season organic garden. Sprouted foods are activated foods, full of life energies and high vitamin contents. They are Live Foods.

*Alfalfa seeds* — These make a delicate sweet salad and sandwich sprout. Use them like lettuce. Buy seeds from a natural foods store; don't use those intended for planting.

*Mung beans/soy beans* — These are the classic oriental bean sprouts, full of superior nutrition. They can be sprinkled in salads or very lightly cooked among other vegetables or sauteed briefly in sesame oil and soy sauce.

*Cooking beans* — Any whole, unhulled, fertile seed will sprout. That includes all types of beans: lima, pinto, black, lentil, aduki, fava, navy, black-eyed peas, etc. After these are sprouted they are fresh vegetables again. Their freshness is accompanied by a terrific increase in the vitamin C content (the freshness vitamin). Steam them with other vegetables (carrots, broccoli, potatoes, onions) and season, or add them to soups and stews.

*Grains* — Whole wheat berries, rye berries, whole oats or brown rice, etc. make delightful sprouts. Their starch converts to sugar and the vitamin C gives a lemony flavor to the sprout. They can be used whole or ground up for breads and soup, or sprinkled in salads.

*How to set up a sprout garden:*
Assemble wide-mouth jars, rubber bands, and squares of non-rustable screen to fit the top of each jar. In a gallon jar, put 1/2 cup of alfalfa seed or a cup of mung or soy beans. For sprouting grains and beans, a gallon jar will hold 2 cups of dry seeds. All these measurements produce a full jar of sprouts.

Fill jar with water halfway and cover it with the screen. After one day, drain the soak-water off, save it for soup stock, or drink it. The soak-water from all sprouted seeds and beans is good in teas and for cooking grains.

Store jars on their sides in a dark place and water and drain the growing seeds twice a day. In four days they will be ready to eat. Sprouts grow faster in warm climates, but will need plenty of water and will mildew if water is left sitting at the bottom of the jar. Set alfalfa and mung sprouts out in moderate light on the final day of growth to pick up chlorophyll.

Sprouts can be used in a wide variety of ways. Here are a few of the ways to enjoy eating sprouts:

*Fruit/Sprout Salad:* Combine in the blender this dressing: 1 cup apple juice, small clove of garlic, enough avocado to thicken. Pour over a salad of alfalfa sprouts, chopped celery or carrot, and pieces of sweet fruits (bananas, papayas, apple, apricot, date, peach, etc.)

*Simple Alfalfa Sprout Salads:*

#1
Bowl of alfalfa sprouts
1 T. corn germ oil
Dash soy sauce
Shredded cabbage (optional)

#2
Bowl of alfalfa sprouts
Chopped parsley
Nut or seed butter

#3
Bowl of alfalfa sprouts
Chopped tomato
Minced garlic
T. pure olive oil

*Tofuna Salad:* Mash with a fork a carton of tofu (soy cheese). Chop very finely the following vegetables: parsley (plenty), onion or scallion, celery and carrot. Add 2 T. soy sauce, 1/2 tsp. kelp powder, 4 T. oil. Mix and use for sandwich spread combined with alfalfa sprouts.

*Far Out Mung Sprout:* Invented to balance amino acids, this is a basic recipe that combines steamed or sauteed vegetables, tofu, and bean sprouts with an aromatic nut or seed butter sauce. Steam a head of cauliflower and three carrots. When almost done, add 1½ cups mung sprouts, 1/2 carton of tofu, 1 large clove of minced garlic, 2 bell peppers, chopped, 1 stalk celery, chopped, 1 cup alfalfa sprouts and 2 T. oil. Add 1/2 cup almond butter, ginger, turmeric, and nutmeg. Season with vegetable salt or soy sauce. Combine all steamed and raw ingredients and stir to develop sauce.

*Able Vegetables*
Steam a pot of assorted vegetables, whole, place denser vegetables closer to the bottom with the quicker-cooking vegetables on top. When half done, add wheat or mung sprouts, green leafy vegies.

Into the serving dish put nuts or seeds, tofu or milk cheese, chopped garlic, peppers, carrot, celery, mushroom, fresh peas or corn kernel to fill 1/4 full.

The cooked vegetables should be firm but not crunchy; cut quickly into bite-sized pieces and stir into the dish. Add a flavorful oil and soy sauce.

There are endless variations to this skeleton recipe: cauliflower, cheddar cheese, parsley and almonds or jerusalem artichokes, onions, mushrooms, tofu and wheat sprouts or carrots, string beans, sweet peppers, zucchini and sunflower seeds, etc.

Again — simple.

*Salad:*
Grate raw beets and carrots
Mix with spinach, sprouts, and celery
Ground seeds and nuts may be added to the raw vegetables as well as garlic, olive oil, and lemon, to flavor.

*Real Cereal*

Granola Style:
2 cups oatmeal
½ cup nutritional yeast
¼ cup honey (optional)
2 cups (combined) of ground corn, rice, and millet
1 Tbsp. kelp powder
Spread ingredients thinly on a baking sheet and bake slowly until lightly toasted. Ground sunflower, sesame, almonds, and pumpkin seeds may be added after baking.

*Peasant Style:*
Place coarse-ground brown rice, corn, millet, oats, buckwheat, and rye in a double broiler or sauce pan. Cook very slowly for an hour.

*Sunflower-sprout cheese:* Place sprouted sunflower seeds in a blender and blend with sesame oil, garlic, and kelp. This mixture may then be spread on sprouted wheat bread, eaten with raw or steamed vegetables or it may be enjoyed all by itself.

# Mothering and Fathering

*Those who love their own children about them; and who are therefore in earnest, will see to it that a right school is started somewhere around the corner, or in their own home.*

*J. Krishnamurti*

The real impact of the play group is in its empowerment of parents. Often parents have such a positive experience they decide to form their own schools. In some neighborhoods this is a necessary response to the racism and sexism inherent in the local schools. Some parents decide to home-school because of their remoteness from a public school. For whatever reason, home-schooling is the fastest growing educational movement in America. It is good that parents are refusing to subject their children to the daily torture of sitting in over-crowded classroom doing what teacher says. Such conditioning leads to tyranny. School should be a place that widens the perimeters of the mind rather than restricts. It should be a place to learn of liberation, not a place of indoctrination. The physical environment of the school should encourage learning.

Children should not come home from school stressed out, shut down and repressed. This is a terrible injustice. A sane and rational government does not permit the destruction of the neighborhood public school system. It is a terrible legacy of feudal days that the quality of education is still largely determined by class and race. It is a sad fact that millions of children from poor neighborhoods routinely graduate from high-school illiterate.

One response to the tyranny is that thousands of creative young people are deciding to go into the teaching profession, (even though it continues to be the most underpaid.) Light is being cast into the stifling halls of the institutions. Some of the more hurtful and repressive modes of teaching are giving way. The good work is happening everywhere. The new breed of teachers is one of the most heartening signs of cultural rebirth.

I have had a great opportunity to learn about the merits of the American educational system. My mother has served the cause of Universal Education for nearly fifty years and is still going strong. She has introduced me to the men and women who have turned inner-city classrooms into bastions of learning. Real learning is possible for all children. Each child deserves to be treated as an individual when it comes to determining their educational program. Each child has special gifts which must be brought out into the light of creativity.

Work and Play

At The Neighborhood School

## Don't Let Them Get Addicted to Television

Regardless of where your child attends school, your example is the most potent educator. Next should come the written, spoken, and sung word. Images associated with words compose the vast unconscious. Do not allow your children to be programmed by the media. Don't leave it to the tube to raise a healthy child. It will not work. Your child needs a wider range of images than the sexually stereotypical television automatons.

Right now, as you read this, millions of children across America are sitting in front of television sets. Many spend seven hours a day watching. Not only is its radiation harmful to their growing bodies, with its phosphorescent light penetrating deeply enough to affect the endocrine system, but it is an "influencing machine", purveying images and ideas which teach all the wrong lessons. While basking in the glow of a television screen, our children's subconscious minds are deluged with disturbing images which condition them towards violence. Children become so captivated by the images on the screen that they often have no idea as to the effect of their viewing. The most potent programming is subliminal. Advertising jingles, which have been designed to "program", are sometimes the only "songs" children assimilate from their culture.

While sitting in front of the television, physical reality is reduced to the abstract dimensions of a hypnotic trance. *No tangible experience occurs.* When the gentle touching inherent in the healthy family is replaced by electronic stimulation and lifeless images, the child's sense of self is compromised. Identity becomes confused with the heroes and heroines on the screen. In 1984 *"Superman"* is still the rage. He still captures the imagination of too many little boys. Young people given television as a substitute for nurturance are finding it extremely difficult to attain genital satisfaction or to maintain cross-gender relationships. This affects family — not only today's family, but the families of tomorrow. Wendell Berry analogizes the television to a vacuum cleaner which sucks the vital force out of the home. As such, it sucks the vital force out of our communities, interfering with our ability to join forces for positive growth and transformation.

Until programming is controlled equally by men and women, and until the values expressed by each gender are oriented towards peace and love, we have got to monitor the use of television. We need not feel guilty about it. Parents must analyze the effect of televison upon their children. There are very few programs that are positively educational. Do not be ashamed to remove it from the home. I know many fine families with happy fulfilled children who do not have magic boxes in their homes; who have books and instruments and participatory playthings in their living rooms.

If television is allowed, it must be backed up by realistic talks about what is being viewed. If violent shows are allowed viewing, they must be counter-balanced with such activities as attendance at peace demonstrations where Vietnam Vets speak. A child counter-balanced may even prove stronger than the child who is merely forbidden televison. But it is far better to forbid than to allow children to be programmed without any intervention.

Children learn self reliance when they witness the people in their life doing good deeds and enjoying the results. Self reliance must be learned. The baby human's tendency to cling and suck never disappears entirely. The tendency is always present. The illusory comforts and securities of materialistic society are a vain attempt to satiate the needs of primal dependency but primal need is too great. And true. It is human to need. In a healthy culture parents teach their children to need God/Goddess. The child learns to surrender to the Dance of Life.

Healthy children naturally grow up to be responsible members of their respective communities. They learn to need, respect, and worship the Divinity in all people. They learn to expand the teachings of their nuclear family to include all of humanity.

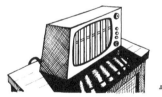

*"The phenomenon of television has the inherent capability (as yet vaguely perceived) of destroying what little integrity of consciousness remains in large numbers of individuals who have developed no resistance to the exhausting demands of living in the mass electronic mainstream of contemporary society.*

*"With the effect of an incredibly subtle drug, television, pulsing its complex signals — which inadvertently link the consciousness of its audience by providing a synchronicity of artificial stimuli in unprecedented quantity, has the insidious potential to effectively anesthetize the Congregational Imperative (the need to gather with others)."*
                                        *Albert Locatelli, Jr.*
                                        *Unpublished Manuscript*

# BOOK THREE
# MATURATION

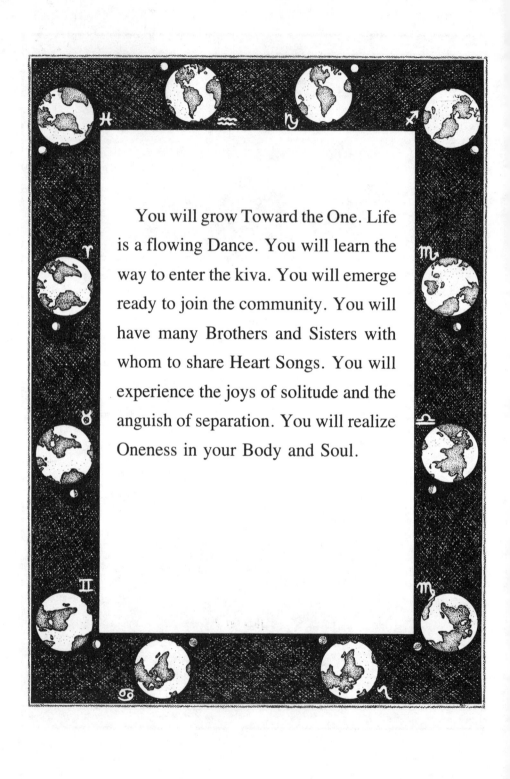

You will grow Toward the One. Life is a flowing Dance. You will learn the way to enter the kiva. You will emerge ready to join the community. You will have many Brothers and Sisters with whom to share Heart Songs. You will experience the joys of solitude and the anguish of separation. You will realize Oneness in your Body and Soul.

# CHAPTER SEVEN

# COMING OF AGE
## Sweetness to Discover

Children need guidance to find the Sweet Road of Life. They must be prepared to be all that they are. When they reach puberty they need you to let go. Indeed, you must encourage their flight from your nest. They are almost ready to fly. But not quite. There is still some time. This limbo produces a great tension and friction from which a golden opportunity may emerge.

While still in the hot house of the nuclear family the teenager needs to learn how to be responsible while the rebellious spirit of life surges through his/her body. This can only happen if parents perceive their childrens' impetus to be liberated from the status quo as a normal, healthy response.

Parenting teen-agers is hard work. It is especially challenging now. The world has never been a more dangerous place for the innocent and trusting. As we approach the Millenium the whole planet will undergo the final stage of the most intense purification that has ever occurred on earth. You must prepare them for the coming changes. Try to see your parenting in a larger perspective. Your job will be much easier if you do not mistake your function. Your job is not to direct your children's lives. Not at this age. They must heed their own call. They hear a Song that is their own. You must trust and respect their Visions.

O' Mothers and Fathers, show your children how to rise in love so that their energies can be utilized for the benefit of all humanity. Encourage them to experience Divinity when they share Love and to let truth guide their sexuality. Empower your children to be glorified in the Golden Egg luminence of the new moon. Teach your daughters how to bleed in the clarity of the void. Guide them forward out of the maze of sexual confusion into the Temple of the Earth-Body. Dance in the light of the Dawn and they will see. And they will grow toward the One Who Gives Life. And they will multiply with pure intention.

To effectively parent your teenage child you must respect their innocence as much as their power. They will seek out and find what they need from the world. Of this you can be sure. Your job as parents is to encourage them to seek truth. This you can only do by example. By living the Golden Rule. By unifying thought and action. By integrating theory with practice. Teach them the Ancient and New, simultaneously. Show them respect for the Word by speaking truthfully. Only by speaking truth will they prosper. Teach them the lessons that can only be learned in the context of a loving family.

The best way to prepare your child for the 21st Century is to be generous and kind. Then they will learn the real work of democracy. Prepare your food wisely. Then they will learn about the Reality of ecology. Illuminate the Four Noble Truths. Then they will know Revolutionary action. Survive with earth wisdom and walk in harmony upon the earth. Then they will learn how to achieve social justice. Clean up after yourself and then they will learn to Respect the integrity of all workers. Each day let them see you pray. Then they will know the One Who Brings Life.

Prepare them for the real work of life, which is to Love. Prepare them to be Lovers of the Sweet Way. Ready them for the powers that will issue forth from their body. Empower them so that they have the strength and dignity to walk the Road of Life.

## Empowerment

Pubescence has an impact upon the developing psyche which is comparable to that of birth and bonding. Even when birth is natural and childhood peaceful, if this transition is disrupted, psychic development is compromised. Dr. James Prescott, in a brilliant work entitled *"Body Pleasure and the Origins of Violence,"* studied 400 different cultures, finding a direct correlation between a low rate of adult violence in societies where there were late weaning, high infant physical affection, low incidence of punishment, and a high acceptance of sexual pleasure. Says Prescott, "These findings overwhelmingly support the thesis that deprivation of body pleasure throughout life — but particularly during the formative periods of infancy, childhood, and adolescence — is very closely related to the amount of warfare and interpersonal violence."

In pubescence we feel the first surge of procreative energy, which will carry us into life's most intense and precious relationships. The urge to care for another brings up the most cherished aspects of human nature. At puberty, the subtle and tender messages which we once felt with our mother, father, and immediate family long to be expressed to others. What a joy it is to have love to share and to know how to reach out with dignity. What a privilege it is to unite with another so that the definitions separating us vanish. Sexual Beings are no longer bound to their mothers and fathers. An essential part of the process of separating from parents is to have love of one's own to express. How exciting it is to make alliances with this love!

Children of both sexes need to be taught the sacredness, as well as the beauty and vulnerability, of sexual energy. They need to respect the Holiness of their bodies. Children of both sexes need to learn that blood-egg-sperm are sacred; that the optimism of God/Goddess is expressed in our seed/egg; that the egg is a manifestation of the Loving Universe.

Positive psychological growth accompanies the physiological changes. When womb blood begins to flow and sperm issues forth, children must be trusted to explore and to find their own ways with their sexual energy. They must experience their pubescent transition in a loving confident way in order to become responsible, sexually active adults. Puberty is the time to begin positive cycles of initiation for our children. It is time that we provide them the greatest possible opportunity for experiencing life. It is time to do away with fears and taboos .

## The Girl-Child at Puberty

The menarche (first menses) clearly marks the transition of pubescence for the girl-child. Until her first flow, she still feels the innocence of childhood, despite the pre-pubescent changes that have been taking place in her body. Her blood flow, however, signals fertility. It opens the doors of motherhood and is integral to her separation from her mother. Her mother's counsel and support are crucial at this time. Clear communication must take place now, especially if it has been lacking in the past. Already mother's unconscious as well as conscious feelings towards men and sexuality have been incorporated into the girl-child's psyche. They will surface at menarche as they never have before.

It is essential that we become aware of our attitudes and practices surrounding menstruation. If fear is involved, there are regenerative repercussions. When fear is associated with either the sensations that arouse pleasure or herald fertility, there is produced a vibrational distortion of the deepest urges of the body.

There are cultures where menstruation is validated as a time of renewal, and thus there is little bloating and cramping or self-destructive irrationality associated with the monthly flow. In these cultures, if such symptoms do occur, the elder women know how to respond to them, usually with healing herbs (see the book Hygieia, A Woman's Herbal, by Jeannine Parvati). These symptoms are signs of easily correctible mineral imbalances.

Monthly renewal is facilitated by women supporting and loving one another during their times of flowing forth. Groups of women who live together link up on primal levels. Their cycles become synchronized via a hormonal scent which is released through the armpit sweat. Because of their potential for synchronicity of cycles, women are attuned to one another during menstruation. It can provide a wonderful opportunity for mothers and daughters to share a special bond. It is a time for mothers to take special care in meeting the dietary and emotional needs of their daughters.

During the menstrual tides, the body is in a vulnerable nutritional balance. This is especially true for the pubescent woman. Pre-menstrual tension is no old wives' tale. It is a result of not only mineral and dietary imbalances but also of blood toxicity. During menstruation, a natural cleansing of the blood takes place. Cleansing can be enhanced by eating wholesome foods and discontinuing all stimulants and drugs. Thus the digestive tract gets a rest and there is a reduction of metabolic stress.

Mothers and daughters who take the opportunity to experience their menstruations together as a time of renewal benefit from not only greater health and well-being but also from a shared bond. Sharing helps to relieve many of the doubts and fears that so often plague pubescent girls and makes the first menses a time of celebration.

Because she feels vulnerable to the changes that have so dramatically taken place, the pubescent girl is extremely impressionable. She will listen to her mother and to other girls and women as she never did before. It is important that mothers and other women offer positive feelings about menstruation, about being "a woman". To do so helps to offset attitudes put forth by our male-terrorized society.

In our society the Holiness of womb blood has been made shameful. The blood is tamponed, deodorized, and extracted. Its sight, smell, and taste are banished from consciousness. The dictates of a male-terrorized society demand that woman's blood be denied. If a girl/woman's first blood is made shameful, she can be conditioned to serve the domestic and sexual needs of men. One has only to observe the governmental chambers of the super powers to know that these men are not monthly cleansed. It is no wonder that their major focus is on ways to shed blood.

Thankfully womanspirit is on the rise and a clear Light is shining from the moon. Today, when a girl's body begins to swell and blood seeps from her womb, she may find support. Many mothers have faced their subconscious fears and so need not pass them on to their daughters; they can acknowledge that their baby girl has a womanly flow — and so a sexual identity all her own. They can counsel with their daughters about creative and positive ways to express their love. Rather than warn and try to protect them out of fear, mothers can use this special time to teach their daughters the many ways of love.

## Mothers and Daughters

Diana Foldvary is the co-author (with Tamara Slayton) of a book (in process) on ways in which mothers can help their daughters' transition in puberty. I asked her to share some of her advice and experience . . .

A group of mothers in the neighborhood, who all had daughters ranging in age from ten to twelve years of age, decided to have a monthly get-together with their daughters. It would be a time to bring up issues and questions which were not easy to talk about at home. Within an environment of fun and friends, these things could be talked about and worked out more easily. As one girl put it, "It's just a lot easier to try to discuss a touchy subject with your Mom when other girls your age are there to show your mom that they too feel the same way." And for the moms, it's a way to get insights from other moms. Everyone feels less isolated with their problems and questions when they see that many others have similar situations to work out.

I was invited to join this group of mothers and daughters one evening. The subject of menstruation had not come up yet and they wanted me to help talk about this. Menstruation is a subject shrouded with taboo. It is a subject that carries with it the shadow of another taboo, that of sex. Both menstruation and sex are laden with confusion, ambivalence, poor communications, and double messages.

I found myself in an interesting and peculiar situation for I had no daughter of my own and could see the dynamics between these moms and their daughters with an objective perspective. I was able to empathize with both the daughters and their moms, and I saw how hard it was for each to see the other's position. It was a struggle.

Within all the conversation I heard echoing an ancient theme. The girls were saying to their moms, "Let us be who *we* want to be; let us try things out so we can choose, and find out who we are." And I heard the echo of the mothers' voices underneath the intellectual response, "but I am so worried that your choices will make you grow different than me, that I am losing my little girl, and that I know better what is good for you at this time." I heard these things echoing under all the talking. The drama of growing up and letting go, the struggle of change, was raging under the fun of the campfire and the bright stars above twinkling with the knowledge of the ages.

The mothers heard the echoes of a voice in their past. They heard their own mother telling them the same thing that they were telling their daughters. They remembered that the arguments their daughters were presenting to them were the same arguments that they had presented to their own mothers. And the stars shone brightly in the cool clear night.

None of the girls in this group had begun menstruating, yet they had a lot of questions and ideas about it. I explained that it is good for them to know about periods now because knowing about it takes a lot of the fear and confusion out of the experience, allowing the momentous day to be truly exciting and wonderful.

The first questions were all about what to wear during one's period and how it feels. I answered these questions about pads, tampons, sponges and glad rags, stating the pro's and con's for each. Most of the girls and moms hadn't ever seen a glad rag, which is a re-usable cloth which folds into a pad. I happened to have one in my purse because I was expecting my period any day. It was made of pink flannel with tiny roses on it. I had used it for two years. Everyone was amazed at how spotless and pretty it was! So I explained about the making, soaking, and wearing of glad rags.

Questions began to pour out. They wanted to know about how much blood to expect and what to do if it came and they were unprepared. I told them that variation is the only true rule regarding cycles and that they may have a very small amount of blood at first or they may have more and both are normal. Little by little fears melted away as answers arrived. We discussed cramps and what to do about them. We talked about diet and the role of health and mental attitude affecting the way one experiences cramps and other menstrual discomforts.

The big fear of getting one's period unprepared and staining one's clothes came up a lot. This question revealed the strong concern the girls had of not wanting anyone to know they were having a period. We talked about how embarrassing it all seems to be, especially with respect to boys or men. I told them that as far as their dads were concerned, they already knew all about it so there really was no secret to keep from them. I said it is about time we begin to feel less ashamed about our bodies and about time we include men and boys in the knowledge of our cycles. At this point, the moms told stories about how even now it sometimes gets awkward to mention they are having their period to a man friend. We wondered who it was that felt more awkward — us or the man? Probably it was us.

After discussing all the aspects of menstruation, one of the girls asked the adults in the group to tell the story of their first period. They wanted to know what it was like for us. So one by one we told our stories. I was first.

# Coming of Age

I told them: "When I was very young, I thought of Pandora, the girl who let all the evils out of her box. I was told that the gods had given Pandora a box as a gift, and she was forbidden to open it. But since it was her nature to be curious, Pandora opened the box and out flew all the evils that the gods had put into the box. It was all a deceitful trick! I had gotten my period recently for the first time and I thought of this box and how my period was one of those things that Pandora must have let slip out. My mother had told me nothing about menstruation although I knew that she had periods because I saw her change pads in the bathroom occasionally. Every month I would see the pads wrapped in newspaper in the trash, with some blood seeping through the paper. It was all very mysterious and somewhat dreadful. I knew some day it would happen to me but that was about all I knew.

Then came the film in school — a cartoon which was very different from the pads in the bathroom. In the film everything was cute and sanitary. There was no blood, just the word 'blood'. I remember the little blonde girl combing her hair in front of the mirror telling us not to worry, and the little blonde girl doing some sort of mild exercise, and the soothing voice telling us how we could still swim but not go horseback riding.

"There were girls in school who had already gotten their periods, discreetly letting the others know, and oh, but it never did show! Then there was the time a girl had to leave the classroom all shamed because she had started her period and a spot was on her dress. She wore her sweater tied around her waist all day to hide it, but she could not hide her face. So when my period came, I expected Pandora's box to open and release all sorts of creepy crawly experiences onto me. Instead, there was one tiny drop of blood on my panties. One little period timidly peeping through. But for me, it was a moment of great importance. So I showed it to my mother and she just said 'Yes, that is your period,' and gave me some tissue to wear as it seemed no more blood was going to come this time. Nothing more was said or done, and I went to my room saddened because I wanted more. I wanted everyone else to know what a big deal this was for me."

The last mother to tell her story was Mary. She told us about how her sister was older than she and already menstruating, and that she got her period only six months after her older sister did. Mary was only ten years old when her period started, and even though she knew what it was all about from her mother and sister, she was shocked when hers came so early. She was a bit unhappy about it because she felt she was too young to be grown up. She recalled how she had been plucking out the few pubic hairs that were growing, hoping that they wouldn't grow

*Annie Laurie dancing, age ten*

back. But they did grow back and her body had decided to begin menstruating.

I ended this story-telling part of the evening by revealing the true nature of the goddess Pandora. You see, before the myth was changed by the people in Greek times long ago, the myth of Pandora was very different. Pandora was the great Earth-Goddess. She is considered the first woman and her name means "the gift of all". In the original myth, Pandora gave to the people of Earth the pomegranate which became the many fruits we eat, and she gave the people of Earth seeds to grow plants for hunger and illness and all the riches of this earth. These were the contents of Pandora's box! Now, since Pandora is the Earth Goddess and our bodies are like the earth, then we too are earth goddesses and our bodies are sacred.

We have come to know through his-story that to bleed is a 'curse', just as Pandora's opening of the box was a 'curse'. But if this story is not true and the box or jar of Pandora brought wonderful things to the earth, then the curse is not a curse — it is a blessing.

The evening was growing late, and the girls and moms were growing sleepy, so we brought the talking to a close, sang a few songs together, and said our good evenings. A few of the mothers and I decided that the next time we met we would begin to discuss creating a ritual or celebration for the first daughter to begin her flow, and for every other girl in her time.

■　　■　　■

**when woman celebrates**
**life flows**
**plants grow**
**people know**
**where they come from**

Michael Markowitz

## The Male Child At Puberty

Due to the more hidden aspects of his sexuality the male child often has no tangible basis or feedback for his initiation into the baby-making phase of his life. The male's ready sperm supply is held and stored in the body in a very different way than the girl's egg. Hers is a cyclical release. His is willed. But the male child needs to be consciously connected to his procreative powers just as tangibly as the girl child is by her blood. When his sexuality is not validated by reality he cannot learn of the power of his seed. As a result, the masturbatory and titillating aspects of sex become the most important, not only in adolescence but in adult life as well.

The sperm is his egg. Like ovulation, male ejaculation is baby-making. Just as the Golden Egg of the Goddess is Holy, so too is his sperm. Sexual energy is Divine Energy. Love is coded into the genital body. It is the force of Love that propels the egg, monthly heals the womb, and builds again the home of conception. It is this same force of Love that builds the sperm. Working with and reconciling this force is a central factor in every man's life. Learning about the nature of sexuality guides one to the altar of Love.

Ejaculation is inherently optimistic. It takes hope to sow. The optimism of ejaculatory orgasm is the most profound sensation of the Body. Male orgasm is entirely different from female orgasm. Although she can climax for hours on end there is only a twenty-four to thirty-six hour period each month when she can experience both ovulation and orgasm simultaneously. For the male, orgasm and baby-making always go together. His psyche is touched by the primal urge of procreation when he "comes."

In order to realize this primal flow, the boy-man must experience the wisdom of his male body. In order for the boy-man to mature into a fully functioning sexual adult, he must integrate his sexual energy within the context of his life. The ultimate reality of earthly life is revealed in his body. The male body is as intimately connected with fertility as the woman's. The moon waxes and wanes in his body as well. There are times of the month when the male is more sexual and times when he, too, needs space to be alone, sleep alone and fast. Finding this place inside takes away the pressure and performance anxiety of sexuality.

In a healthy culture, boys and girls have a community of support that both honors their passages from one stage of life to another and guides them into healthy cross-gender relationships. As his sexual power begins to rise, the male child needs to be included in open and loving dialogue with wiser males. Never is the appreciation and validation of men more important than when we are first testing out the waters of our manliness. We need the guidance of sexually healthy men.

The force of pubescence is too tremendous to handle alone. We are so tender! As we discover the pleasure of orgasm we want to share our feelings. But society does not sanction healthy sexual exchanges between boys and girls. Pubescent girls know less about the male body than their own. They are often disgusted by sperm. And yet there is this driving force of energy that continues to rise in his genitals. And so he masturbates. He masturbates in his mother's house. He does it in his socks, towels, anywhere where there will be no trace. His sexuality and sperm are demeaned. He doesn't even know it but rejection of his sperm deeply affects his consciousness. Ask any man how it feels to have a woman "go down on him" and then pull her mouth away when he is about to come. The only reason a man can tolerate such demeaning sexuality is that he has been "well trained" in his early years.

Just look at the way boys walk down high school halls. So cool! But the price paid for repression is loss of sensitivity. The boy does everything to hide his nakedness. Inside he feels as if a cocoon is being stripped away. Childhood is over and now comes the severe test of manhood. And so we get cool, tough, "bad". The model of sexuality is the cool, horny man. Pursuit becomes the goal and the harmony and bliss of sexual sharing are lost.

It is essential for the boy-man to learn that it is not necessary to have an erection to be intimate. It is possible to share love without being driven by the hot tip of the penis. Hot-genital sexuality often sublimates creative energy. The boy-man needs to learn it is possible to cuddle without coming, to be naked without darkness, to be Holy in the flesh, to delight in the flesh with dignity and honesty.

Sexual energy is Divine. The purpose of sex is to generate Love. Sexual release is an external expression of a revolutionary urge for deeper levels of reality. When boys learn to listen to their bodies, they turn into men who can hear the call of the Holy Spirit within their Temple.

To grow sexually wise the male must learn certain truths about the moon and his body. He must learn the root nature of desire and learn how to charm the coiled snake at the base of his spine. In the New Age, men develop a profound respect for the energy that lives within their Body. They are aware of how they extend and increase that energy. They learn to play without getting numbed and to contain without turning off. They are able to experience ecstatic sexuality as well as ecstatic celibacy. They are free to Be. And to feel what it is to live and cycle in a male body.

Part of growing up is learning about the effect of the moon on the sperm-cycle. The boy-man learns to use his sperm as an ally. As medicine. As Gods' own homeopathic remedy. The knowledge of such usage is common to all advanced systems of medicine. (Note: We are discussing the use of one's own sperm, not in homosexual ingestion). This Ancient knowledge is coming back. A few are beginning to speak of the taboos.

I had a chance to speak to the Rainbow Shaman Rob Menzies, author of *Star Herbal,* about the male-moon cycle. This conversation took place on the Vernal Equinox of 1980.

**Menzies:** The minute that the man starts to eat of his sperm, there are *many* things that start to happen on a procreative level, including the re-establishment of zinc reserves.

Zinc is only produced in the testes, and only the woman gets the zinc. The man loses zinc, yes. It actually weakens the man over a period of time and those of us, as men, who break the taboos, who start to look at our sperm, our kundalinic life force or our procreative, progressive life force in an intellectual manner, see that life force as something that should not just be whacked off in the hand and put in a sock and idly cast away to be laundered by Mom. But it should be looked at from the spiritual — you know, ''what is this?''

**Joshua:** A woman has an egg released once a month. That's her procreative substance. Male and female orgasms are very different. The woman does not ''come with eggs'', her orgasm doesn't ''ooze eggs''. The male does and it sets up a very different dynamic between the male and female.

**Menzies:** ''Oozing eggs'', I love this! We ''ooze'' sperm. Physical man has got to look at his cycle, too. I do have a cycle. I'm using the moon as a cycle guide. I've been doing this now, oh, I'd say, since about '75.

**Joshua:** And what are you finding?

**Menzies:** I find that I *am* on a cycle. That my body odors change, my attitude changes, my food needs change, my urine, my sperm, everything!

Joshua: So do you feel that you have a period of the month when your . . .

Menzies: Yes, I do! Definitely, it is a cleansing. I am also making tinctures with the menstrual bloods and I am adjusting of the menstrual bloods. There are only specific times of the cycle that I can "be" with. When I'm with an Indian, I cannot be at all; when with a "white" I can be once in awhile. I'm very conscious of this, very aware of these places.

Joshua: How can men who are not living on the earth begin to get more in touch?

Menzies: I think the first way is to wash their hands in their water, to break a taboo. To smell themselves, to look at themselves, to put themselves in a jar. To get that ego out, to really smell yourself. I mean, after all . . .

Joshua: Beautiful.

Women know much more about the ramifications of fertility than men. The female body is keyed into the moon. She must pay strict attention to her blood. If she does not bleed she worries. Or is elated. Her fertility cycle has a direct bearing on her life. Ovulation and menstruation define the ebb and flow of her cycle. Weaving the Golden Egg is central to the way her Body works.

Both male and female are revived by the power of procreation. But a woman only ovulates once a month. A man can will his ejaculation anytime. However he ejaculates, the creative-love-juices flow. It does not matter if there is a rubber covering his penis or if he is in a gay bar. He can will his seed forth. He can will the Divine into his body. The male has a great responsibility coded into his procreative urges.

It is very difficult to find sexually wise men. We have so many extreme examples of male sexual energy: The rigid celibate who takes a vow, withholds his sperm, and segregates himself from the company of women; the swami who f--ks his young female disciples in the middle of the night and lectures on seminal retention in the daytime; the escapades of the singles clubs and gay bars.

The healing man discovers what is really happening within his own body. For some men, during periods of singleness and healing, masturbation may be the best way to affirm life force. The healing man learns how to make love with himself. This is a natural phase of growth. The way a man masturbates is indicative of his sexuality. It is essential to pay attention to one's thoughts while masturbating as well as to how one feels afterward. It is also important to honor the seed so cast. Taste your sperm. Spread it on your body. For God's sake just don't whack it off and wipe it up. This is a precious gift. Think of God as you ejaculate.

The new man is challenged to clarify whether his urge for sexual union is genital or mental. The two are only compatible when the Heart is the intermediary. Oftentimes a man's desire for sex is a need to relieve himself of toxicity. The physical act of ejaculation is a means to purify the body. When a man's liver and kidneys become overloaded with the acids of protein indigestion, the lymph system takes over the efforts of elimination. When this avenue is exhausted, the body resorts to seminal fluid. In other words, the man may use ejaculation much like menstruation. It is essential to learn how to transmute these feelings rather than project sexual energy in destructive ways.

Many creative men masturbate periods of solitude away. Seed casting becomes a daily routine. To break the habit it is helpful to eat lightly, especially of sperm producing foods such as meat, lentils, eggs, nuts, and cheeses. It is also very helpful not to eat after six p.m. The solar plexus and genitals are bathed in the same blood. Pressure on the abdominal wall creates tension in the genitalia. Most of all it is essential to remember who you are when you ejaculate.

Remember brothers, beneath the leather jackets and petticoats there is a Divine Source which both genders share. For a man to serve God with his seed he must learn new ways to dance. This is the time to pray and wait. Be thoughtful and discriminating. Ponder the realities of the secret garden. Experiment wisely.

Wait for someone special. And then fly on the wings of Truth and Love. Plant your seeds with Love, brother. Only with Love. Heed the call of the original urge within your Body-Temple. Heed the good deeds of the Holy. Be Holy when you get naked.

If you find yourself falling in love or know you need guidance, gather five Brothers together and seek a vision. New Age men exalt the Spirit with the power of their love.

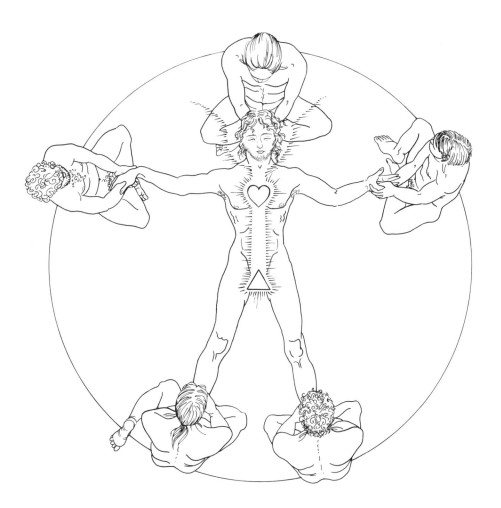

## Vision Quest: The Key To Positive Change

As the sexual fire begins to manifest, both male and female have a deep need to expand their horizons as well as to perceive inner reality. The pubescent transition entails finding one's own way. There is a certain amount of rebellion inherent and appropriate to this stage of life. A healthy culture respects and encourages rebellion. Out of the fresh energy of the young come the visions of the future. Truly, if the youth would go to the tops of mountains to seek Vision, this war-torn world could be a love-filled Garden.

When the power to bring forth new life is activated within the body, there is a need to face and challenge mortality. To be able to give birth one must be able to "die". The two learnings go together in the experiential quest of the human psyche for wholeness and transcendence.

As the sexual power builds in the body, there is a great need to process the past and move on. All of the subconscious material of infancy rises to the surface when one is vulnerable to the sexual feelings of the body. Coming into adulthood, one discovers internal life. It is not enough to merely acquire the car, motorcycle, drugs, football emblem, electric guitar, ring. It is not enough to merely act out the new feelings. The force of new life needs to be taken within and listened to. This is a time to pray, seek guidance. Every young man and woman has a need to seek out the truth of their lives.

At puberty, there is a life-truth that longs to be revealed. All young people want to feel at peace with their world. No young person that I have ever met really "got off" on a drunken revelry or narcotic stupor. The dulling of the mind through substance abuse and angry defiance is a result of denied inner needs. A healthy culture must learn to hear inner needs. The clarity of youth must be respected. The creative energy of the young is wondrous. It must be honored and channeled into positive ways of Being.

The vision quest is one of the best ways for pubescent boys and girls to work through this intense time. A Vision Quest is a ceremony which provides the participant with a challenging, yet defined, space in which to change, grow, and integrate. It is a ceremony that sheds light on one's daily life. For the first time, shadows may be faced and conquered.

The quest is an antidote to suicidal motorcycle rides and teenage pregnancy. It is a time when a young man/woman may find the drumbeat of his/her life.

I asked Steven Foster, author of *Vision Quest,* about his pioneering work in this field . . .

*One of the weaknesses of modern Anglo-European culture is its inability to provide legitimate and sanctioned "growth events" or "experiential education" for youth entering adulthood. Like youth of traditional societies, modern youth also require 'growing up' experiences (beyond the driver's license or the age of 21) which 'certify' or 'credential' them to be adult, in their own eyes, and in the eyes of their parents, relatives, and peers.*

*An ancient, time-proven, formal ceremony of the experience of passing from youth to adulthood, the vision quest contains many learning ingredients that have been removed (vacuumed) from "adolescent" education. These ingredients include the experiencing of the fears of loneliness, hardship, starvation, the unknown, boredom, living without Mother/Father,and learning of personal ability to deal with such fears on emotional and physical levels. This rite of passage affords youth an opportunity to plan, prepare for, experience and master these fears in a formal setting, with the official sanction of parents, family, significant others, peers.*

*The vision quest contains an added ingredient rarely found in modern education of youth. It engenders spiritual and/or ethical learning and strengthening within the personal religious or mythical framework of the individual, and this prepares him/her to deal with the hardships and crises of adult life. Without this added ingredient, modern life is empty of meaning and direction.*

The following stories are from the Vision Quest Book.

The gift to give, the trail to follow, is revealed to the hero/ine when the eyes are opened and the quester sees with the eyes of eternity. The name of the gift is no secret: the gift of love. But it is one thing to know about love; it is another to see with the eyes of eternity. The modern hero/ine, living in a mythically impoverished culture, is nevertheless capable of experiencing mystical insight, of seeing with opened eyes what it is that binds the self and all things together in oneness.

The following account clearly indicates the mythical potential of the Vision Quest. Not everyone, however, is necessarily gifted with the ability to experience mystical insight. For reasons known only by the Great Mother, this young heroine was given one of life's greatest prizes.

January 2.

Night came on. I built no fire. I placed my rocks into a circle starting at north, then south, to east, then west. Each time I set a rock in its place, I gave my cry: "Dear Father, We need!"

I let my mind drift, with no preconceptions of what I would see. Little happy memories came to me. It seemed that my childhood was suddenly unfolded before me. I saw my growth through the sadness and joy experienced in that past. I felt at peace, content with the spirit I had become. I no longer felt that parts of my past should have been different. Then came the little images. I got so tired that I dozed off: two, fifteen, thirty minutes at a time.

In one image, I saw a candle burning. It slowly transformed itself into an old-fashioned kerosene lamp, then into a light bulb. History, eternal ideas, the promise of the progress of Love— I felt them all.

I saw a bright, fiery ball, There was a black hole in the middle of it. I felt my whole being rushing, as if vacuumed, toward that hole. I entered it. Blackness all around me. So peaceful. The feeling of being received, accepted. I opened my eyes. I was *here*, on Earth! I realized that that image symbolized my Passage. I was born to this exciting, beautiful, ugly, dangerous, receiving Earth.

But why have I denied this feeling of becoming one with the world? I have been so afraid of feeling naked, stripped of my status, my security from home, my pride, my old confidence, my feeling I controlled the world around me. . . . Those things were my supposedly indestructible foundation. But as I am learning from the mountains, eventually what seems to look like a secure, sturdy rock will crumble under too much force. Someday it will succumb.

I looked at the moon—a glowing crescent. I actually saw a pure, shining dove rise out of it and descend to Earth! I had my eyes wide open. I saw that beautiful bird flying down toward the planet. I closed my eyes and screamed: "Dear Father, We need!" I thought that the image was a hallucination. I was afraid to believe in such a powerful sight.

Then it clicked. I was sitting there in my bag in the blackness. My head was tilted up toward the sky and stars, and my eyes were closed. I began to feel raindrops on my closed eyelids. Then, still with my eyes shut, I saw triangular, no, pyramid-shaped figures of light traveling from every direction, heading for my eyes, going through my eyes into my soul. I felt a surge of power, of awareness.

I opened my eyes. Those brilliant stars were still sending down pyramids of energy to me—I saw it all clearly. Like a river, there was a

constant flow of that warmth, power and light coming directly from the stars into my being through my eyes.

Everything just seemed to click. The Spirit (I call it God) sent me that mystical message: Love. He gave me that reason why I'm here on earth. This wonderful planet gives us the place to not only exist as a life form, but to grow together. I'm here to participate in that potential fellowship. I'm here to Love and accept. Through those images—the stars, the sun, all this energy in the world—I can collect it within me, and direct it to humanity.

The hero/ine enters the threshold incomplete. Via the solitary heroic journey through the body of the Great Mother, the seeker is healed, made complete. The gift cannot be given to others until the self is whole and well. Love cannot be imparted until the self is loved.

Sometimes the dragon to be encountered is lack of self-love, that is, self-destructive behavior, particularly those which are addicting, is not won in a single fracas. The dragon appears and reappears to claim its victims, and the only way to fight it is with the rage of love and self-respect. Words and high intentions are not sufficient.

The hero/ine engages the dragon of self-destruction in a battle. By learning how to win, the seeker learns how to live. Learning how to live, the seeker learns how to die.

Graham, the hero of the following story, is living today in Marin County. He engaged the dragon of self-destruction during a Vision Quest to Nevada several years ago. He may never be entirely free of his dragon, but he crossed the threshold and was given the gift of wellness, of completeness. He saw what he had to do. Then, fearful as any hero, knowing all too well the gigantic proportions of his own personal dragon, he stepped back across the threshold to do battle.

## GRAHAM

He was a nice guy—and he was a heroin addict. He was in a therapeutic community of ex-junkies when he first heard about the Vision Quest. From the beginning he was the most enthusiastic about stretching his muscles and living alone with the forces of Nature. All his counselors said it would do him good.

Socially he was a star, a vital, magnetic man who spoke candidly and with intelligence. But nobody knew what he would do when he left the support system and friends of the therapeutic community and went back alone to the streets of San Rafael, where his old junkie friends were still lurking for a fix, anxious to prove he was no better than they.

So he went to the headwaters of the Reese River in Nevada's Toiyabe Mountains with a bunch of other friends from the therapeutic community, with his counselor, Al, and a nurse, Angela (to dispense methadone to those who required it). While he was there he took to the mountains like a snake to a warm rock. He caught his limit of Rainbows and Eastern Brooks with worms he scavenged from the banks of Upper Sawmill Creek. He slept in the hollow of a willow tree. He hiked up the ravines and came back with arrowpoints in his hands. He ate like a horse and slept like a lamb. "This is the life for me," he declared, and talked about becoming a cowboy. If he was a star in his therapeutic community, he was a blossom in the high desert.

When he came back from his Vision Quest, he seemed bigger than life. It had been a good time for him, a time of self-testing and self-analysis. The late summer sun was strong and pure. It burned the impurities from his body. The fasting cleansed him from within. He had picked wild rosehips from the bushes growing near the river and made strong, sweet tea. His eyes were clear and alert, like an animal's; his body was lean and brown. He looked damn good.

That night, after the giving away and the numerous stories, he announced that he was not going back. The city held no more interest for him. He would stay here, maybe hire on at one of the ranches down in the valley.

We talked about going back then, for a long time, as the fire exhaled sweet juniper and the stars danced their slow ballet across the sands of forgetful night. The real monster, we decided, was fear of going back to face the monster.

The next morning we hiked out. It was a sad time. As we ascended the canyonside, the river glistened like a green snake shedding a skin of willows. "I'll always remember what I learned here," vowed Graham.

A month later he graduated from the therapeutic community and went to live in San Rafael, working up in Petaluma cleaning out chicken coops. He rode the bus to and from work, came home exhausted every night. He took up with his old girl friend, the same one who had first introduced him to heroin. He told us he was staying clean.

I went over to his place a couple of times. It was a depressing apartment with no windows and a TV set at one end. At the other end was a shrine: a little picture-altar with a deer skull, a pair of antlers, obsidian flakes, and photos and mementos of his Vision Quest. He talked vaguely about getting out to Pt. Reyes or up to Yosemite, but he seemed full of inertia and sodden with self-disgust at the grind he found himself in. He smoked a lot.

A couple of months later, I read about him in the newspaper. He and his old lady had been caught with stolen goods and an "undisclosed quantity of heroin." He was back in jail, back where he had started.

For a long time I heard nothing of him. Then three years later he passed me on the freeway. He was driving an old but respectable pickup truck with a tool box in the back. "Hey," he yelled excitedly. "Hey!" I yelled back at him, "how're you doing?"

He hung his head out the window with a big grin on his face and hollered, "I'm clean!"

■    ■    ■

## Returning from the Quest

When you return the first thing you want to do is tell everyone. But this is the time for silence. Stay quiet with your changes. You have just begun. Talk about change should only be with those who know more than you do. Life is for living. Be aware of the inertia of the past. There will be many forces that will try to take you from the Path. This commodity-crazed world will try to suck you back into confusion. You will find a million alibis for abandoning your vision. But do not. Keep to the center. Listen to the sound of intuition. The Holy Spirit is guiding you. By finding your roots you now belong to the future. Keep on listening to the One-Heart. Take time everyday to remember your vision.

After the Vision Quest you must fit back into the world with a new perspective. One always returns with more responsibility. This is the nature of the search for Source. The more one empties oneself of false accumulations the more one is ready for the real work.

Our work is cut out for us. One doesn't have to travel far to find good work to do or people to study with. There is so much to learn, so much rebuilding to do. We have a nation to mend. This is the time to draw on your real power and reach out your hand. Gather with your brothers and sisters and be grateful for each day.

Don't grumble about what isn't. Do something about it. Go study with a wandering monk. Apprentice with a midwife or husband. Rise in love with a Best Friend. Start a storefront clinic or a natural foods restaurant. Teach first grade in the ghetto. Go to the farms and apprentice with masters of the soil. Seek out the wise herbalists, naturopaths, and barefoot doctors. Go to college and seek the wise professors who have managed to endure the stifling confines of the academy. Become members of a neighborhood and community. Study hard. Most of all find your innate talents and chart a course that will allow them to blossom. Find the way that your Ancestors dreamed of.

Fit yourself into a larger and larger perspective of the world. Expand your roots to other lands and peoples. Learn the songs of other tribes. Learn to take communion in many Houses of Worship. Remember that you belong to the Earth, to the soil upon which you stand. Bend down daily and give thanks to the Heavenly Father.

Once you've been to the Mountain you've got to come back to the Valley and share what you know with your brothers and sisters. Going to the mountain is not for one's own salvation. It is for all of us. Whenever anybody breaks free it benefits us all. Once you've been to the Mountain your roots will find the Source of Life. This is the time for communion. After union comes communion. Once the essential oneness of life is discovered it is only natural to join with others in the celebration of life.

Orient yourselves in the direction of Life. Live fully in the Body of your Earth. You are a Child of the Universe. All Children come from the Tree of Life. All Children are Holy. Know this. Do not judge yourself by the dictates of duality. The days of fear are over. Now is the time to gather in the Light of Creation.

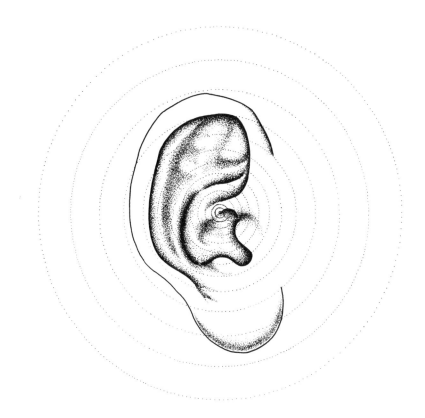

# CHAPTER EIGHT

# LIVING IN THE FREE WORLD
## Gather Together

Hear the Freedom Songs being sung in your neighborhood. The Voice crying out from the wilderness of your Heart is Ancient. You are not singing alone. There is a whole choir singing. All over this Earth the Children are calling out for Freedom. Freedom is the Grace of Being. Freedom is the water that nurtures the Roots of the Soul. Freedom is the rarest and most endangered form of Life on the Planet.

The fish have the seas and the birds the air but the Children of the Earth must struggle hard to get to the Freedom Land. And getting there is just the first step. To remain Free one must live in accordance with the Laws of the Universe. Freedom is only found by those who are concerned with the totality of experience. This is especially true, as we approach the Millenium.

The whole planet has been interconnected by the Aquarian mind of God. It is time for the wars to end. The destruction must end. The truth has set us free. We know how many babies are starving to death today. And we are doing something about it. We know what is being done to the Rain-Forests. We know all about the waste dumps of Babylon. We have watched generations succumb to psychic numbing. We have witnessed the sexual plague. We know the newspapers lie. We have seen backstage. There has been ample opportunity to learn from the mistakes of the past. It is time to bring out the ceremonial drum.

In the Free World, Heaven and Earth bring about the Revolution. The Revolution is Divine. The seasons change of their own accord. It is Spring time on the Earth planet. The Tree of Life is Blossoming. All over the Planet the Children are rising in love. All over the Earth the Children are calling out for their Freedom. Are learning to call out. Are daily calling. All over this sweet Earth the Children are uniting in the Light. In the Free World the people gather in circles and praise the Return of the One-Sun.

In the Freedom Land the people join together and make communities where they live in harmony with the Sun and Moon. In the Free World the Sun and Moon are married inside the Body Temple each and every morning. A free people live on an Earth that has a definite path around the Sun. A free people intuit what is coming. A free people are a wise people. They know Earth is their Home. And they love To Be in the Garden.

Praises Be! In the Free World there are always large groups of people in Prayer and Meditation. In the Free World there are always large groups of people gathering to set the Tone, to listen to the Sacred Call of Silence. Celebrations of Life happen all the time in the Free World. Here there is no dichotomy between Spirit and Matter. In the Free World the Prayer Warrior leads the charge and the whole community is in tune with the Return of Light.

The point is to know freedom as a tangible and accessible part of your life. It is not something abstract. Not at all. It is here and now. Always. It is within you. No tyranny can take it away. Freedom is not a choice. It is a demand of being human.

## Freedom Begins At Dawn

If you listen to the Teachers of Wisdom, you will hear a consistent message: Prayer keeps the Sun returning. The Wise Ones knew that when an individual, community, and nation pray with the power and freshness of the dawn, it impregnates them with a Love that is stronger than any man-made weapon, or ideology. With the rising sun Creation is renewed.

To be born again is an ongoing process. Salvation and Liberation are not one-shot deals. To be born again is to be liberated from the shackles of mental slavery, from the grossness of lust and gluttony, from the petty dictates of matriarchal/patriarchal consensus. To be born again is to be awakened daily and renewed on the altar of life. Liberation and Salvation are about being bonded to the Eternal and Earthly. Redemption is to be found in Creation, on Earth. In this Body.

In this Body, on this Earth, the Sun never sets. There is always a newborn babe emerging from the blisswaters, a lover reaching out in tender embrace. On this Earth, in this body, optimism is never false. There is always the Dawn. A strong people hold fast to the Good News of the One-Heart. A united people always Remember the Grace of Life.

The morning prayer is a calling out to God/Goddess, but it is not an other-worldly event. It enables us to more fully love the people we meet in the morning. To awaken in the morning with a dream song to share with those who eat at your table brightens up the world. To awaken in the morning ready to share in sacred worship lightens the world. This is one of the most effective tools we have to establish community.

The finest gift that any child can be given is that of a mother and father who wake up in the morning cheerful and glad that a new day has begun. When children see and feel their parents starting the day off happily, it validates their own deep spirituality. It is the nature of children to be happy in the morning and to praise the glory of life in its simplicity and splendor. One of the great blessings of living with young children is to experience the wonder and renewal they feel each day.

The ability to be optimistic in the morning, regardless of one's age, status, and romantic or physical condition, is the greatest freedom. To be able to align oneself with joy requires a degree of maturation that denotes a positive and clear outlook within. Only from within can the light shine forth. The morning prayer helps us to shine forth, to be happy, to feel good about living, to feel the blessing, the gift, of another day.

The morning prayer is both preventative and regenerative. With prayer, we are less likely to abandon ourselves in empty pursuits throughout the day and more likely to hold on to that which has intrinsic, lasting value. The morning prayer creates an auric white light of protection around us. The morning prayer unites us, integrates and validates our entire beings. It lifts us from the womb of sleep into the grace of dawn.

When we emerge from the darkness of night into the light of day with gratitude in our hearts, it enables us to speak kindly, gently, and with awareness. To be reborn with the dawn neutralizes the accumulations of the past, and uproots terror from the fiber of our being. To be attuned to the birth light with grace in our hearts allows healing to enter our beings.

When we seek the "Source" at Dawn a channel is opened up for receiving the Divine. This is why many people desire to engage in sex first thing in the morning. To birth themselves, they tap into the energy through which they were conceived. How we feel when we first awaken in the morning is our birth. It is very comforting to be sexual at this time. One of the principal reasons many men find living alone intolerable is that they cannot "get it" when they awaken with an erection.

A healthy man wakes up with an erection. In many cross-gender relationships, women make love to their partners to get them out of the house and off to work. Do not fall into this pattern. It is essential for new age lovers to pray before sex. To pray before ejaculation. To pray before opening up your Temple. Before entering into communion, center into the Core of your Body and swim on the waves of each breath. Awaken as you dive into the procreative waters of Creation, awaken as you play in the fields of the Lord. Awaken as you cuddle in the Garden. The purpose of sexual love is to awaken. The purpose of sexual love is to learn that the positive vibrations of orgasm exist in each moment.

## Mid-day Praises

Each day when the sun is at its peak, be conscious of receiving Light. Ground the energy pulsating through your body. Introspect. Buddha ate his one meal at noon. For many it is the best time to eat one's main protein-rich meal. Families who share this meal together have the opportunity to give thanks to the Light, which births us all.

At noon, as the sun reaches its zenith, take time to feel the fullness of Light. Be pregnant every day. Everyday is a glorious opportunity to walk upon this earth. Pause for a moment and let your gaze be free in the natural light. Feel the Light of God fill you and know that God is ruling the Sun. The sun shines for all. God is for all of us equally. Seize the sun from the sky and set your intention on the Unification.

## Evening Prayers

Each night put an aura of white light around your family. See them all in peace. In-vision them healthy and well. By so praying the night Eagle flys and the Sun is beckoned.

Prayer at dusk integrates the stored-up impressions of the passing day so that we may peacefully enter the womb and emerge refreshed.

Just fifteen minutes of silence before sleep can release the stress of the day. Let renewal occur. Sometimes a brisk walk beneath the stars or graceful dancing in the living room is what our being needs. Indeed, such practices are of greater benefit to restful sleep than the tons of tranquilizers and sleeping pills taken each month by our insomniac nation.

Another effective practice before rest is journal-keeping. Especially beneficial is drawing mandalas of free-form patterns that express our sense of the day. Add a few accompanying words with the drawings to make a multi-media statement of the day's experience — an illustrated koan.

The dusk prayer prevents the accumulation of unresolved resentments, anxiety and despair from following us into the private world of sleep. It demarcates what we wish to take into bed with us. It is an act which sanctifies the ground we rest upon.

Of course, there is a responsibility that accompanies prayer. Praying results in a power that cannot be hoarded. It must be expressed. Love is the thread that weaves us all together. The morning, mid-day, and evening prayers enable us to be competent weavers — to build a larger and larger family. Let the power of your prayers draw you together so that the family you belong to includes the Nature Spirits as well as all of Humanity. Let the protection enable you to give your best to people in your everyday life.

## For Health and Happiness at Any Age
## To be Taken Daily as Directed:

1. *Upon rising, do a few gentle stretching exercises, breathing deeply through the nose.*

2. *Do some simple, practical thing with your own hands. Work in the garden; hang clothes on the line; bake, sew; carve; draw a picture for a friend.*

3. *Take a long, vigorous walk in the fresh air. Get to know the flowers and trees, insects and animals, children and neighbors. Walk tall, in good posture.*

4. *Close your eyes. Relax. Take a nap. Give yourself a few minutes of complete relaxation every day.*

5. *Establish a harmonious rhythm of living. Go to bed before you are overtired. Rise before the sun is too high in the sky. Avoid taking on more work or responsibility than you can comfortably handle.*

6. *Live a life of moderation. Eat in moderation. Sleep in moderation. Drive in moderation. Watch television in moderation. Work in moderation. Play in moderation.*

7. *Think and act positively. Laughter, smiles, and kind words are powerful medicines. Feeling good is contagious. Infect other people with your own health and happiness.*

*Suevo Brooks*

Let our prayers bond us so that we may journey forth together. Pray out loud that the Children may hear the Eternal Call. Listen to the Silence of God.

A new day is coming. When you rest for the night you will go safely into the darkness. Each night you will wind down the little tunnel with the white light at the end. Each night you will die and be cleansed of the past. Each day you will awaken strong and ready to do your work. You will let the Light call you in from the night. You will rise with joy. Another day to work in the Garden. Another day to live the Golden Rule.

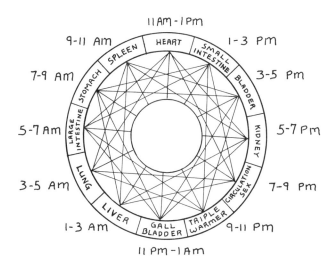

*Let the Wheel of Life Circle You Kindly*
*And The Pure Light Within You*
*Guide Your Way Home*

## Family and Friends Share the Sabbath

Setting one day a week aside to gather with others is an important force in the regeneration of culture. Gathering with a vital
group of people and praising life is soul food of the highest order.
It is not a luxury food, or a supplement to be taken when one is dy-
ing. Gathering together in the communion of a larger family is as
necessary to the development of whole human beings as all the
rest of the biological transitions we have discussed throughout
this book. The human organism is regenerative, but it needs communion. Meeting in communion enriches the internal life of the individual. We need to collaborate with others on a weekly basis.

The orientation and focus of the group may vary. For some, it
may be a Church, Temple, or other Spiritual gathering force. For
me, now, Sabbath begins with and involves my weekly midwifery
studies. At our Friday meetings, we always begin with song and
circle. Then we delve into current events, birth reports, and an in-
depth study of an aspect of midwifery. We end as we began, with
songs in the circle. This circle is full of children, many of them on
the breast and many still inside the blisswaters. It is a very fertile
circle, a circle that generates much Light. For me, it is a vital part
of my weeklife.

I asked Reuven Goldfarb, of the Aquarian Minyan, to share his
perceptions about weekly gatherings for family and community.
His story is a beautiful example of how family and friends share
the Sabbath.

## HOW OUR OBSERVANCE OF SHABBAT
## INFLUENCES OUR FAMILY LIFE

My wife and I first met at a weekly Kabbalat Shabbat (receiving of the
Sabbath) celebration and came together in the context of a newly forming Jewish community in Berkeley, California. It has been our usual
practice since we met, both before and after our marriage, to attend
these Friday night gatherings at people's homes, meet with friends
there, and pray with them in an egalitarian Minyan (quorum of worship-
pers). It is our constant practice to at least read the Torah portion of the
week the following morning if no formal service was planned by our
group.

Since infancy, our children, now 5 and 2½, have been welcomed and encouraged to participate by other Minyan members and visitors. They always look forward to and enjoy attending these and other religious and cultural events that we sponsor.

At times, children's noisemaking, *non sequitur* questions and remarks, and general restlessness in contrast to adult rhythms have been a problem for adults. Most of the members are single people who are alternately fascinated and inconvenienced by children. We have dealt with this problem by insisting that we should not take sole responsibility for our children's behavior. A voice level that is tolerable for us might seem outrageous to somebody else, and we did not want to have to anticipate what someone else's level of discomfort might be. Thus, we asked people to address the children directly if they are made uncomfortable by what they are doing. The adults were relieved to learn that we would not be insulted to have someone else correct our children in our presence.

As a consequence of this mutually open attitude, our children have continued to form strong bonds with many of the adults and other children in our Minyan and regard several of them as older friends, or at least enjoyable companions. Of course, they especially like the loud singing and vigorous dancing that are often part of our services, but they can appreciate the quieter moments too — the meditations, rituals (like candlelighting and kiddush) and silent prayers, as well as the personal sharing that precedes our service — during which time everyone is given a chance to speak, including the children. They also like the food (vegie potluck) which follows the service. Yum!

Saturdays are usually at-home days for us. We do not drive then and we only rarely attend synagogue services, unless it is also a major Holy Day, and then our Minyan creates its own event. It's a non-work day, with special restrictions to protect the sacred time: no phone calls in or out, likewise with T.V., radio, phonograph, and the opening of mail. We hang out a lot together — reading the portion of the week and the Haftorah with its commentaries, using the time we make available for study, prayer, and reflection. Our children are free to move in or out of our space and we accommodate ourselves to their needs, within reason. They are allowed to play on the block with other kids but not take automobile excursions, even if invited.

We make a lunch (Second Meal) with minimal food preparation — I don't make pancakes or hot cereal on Shabbat, and usually have various cold sandwich combinations along with left-overs from Friday night. We make kiddish and motzi (the blessings over wine — or grape juice — and read) and eat. A Shabbos nap for everyone is an important part of the day. The children take daily naps, but we (Yehudit and I) usually do not. Shabbat, however, is a chance to rest from the week's toil, so we gladly comply with these health-giving and life-maintaining customs. Afterwards, there is usually time for a walk to the playground, giving all of us a chance to work off some physical energy.

We come home after an hour or two, have another meal, sit quietly, talk leisurely, and enjoy the "dreaming space" of *Seudah Shishit* (Third Meal). Shabbat ends when three stars are visible at one glance, and it becomes a kind of game to see who can observe the signs first. Yeshayah, my five-year-old boy, has exceptionally good vision and usually notices them first. We then make Havdalah, a ceremony marking the separation between the seventh day and the six working days. It involves a braided candle with several wicks close together so that their flames merge. For me it symbolizes the closeness Shabbat brings to our family since on Friday night, when candles are also lit, they stand in separate holders, and each member of the household lights his or her own.

We bless the wine, but do not drink it yet. We then bless the spices, pungent or sweet-smelling herbs placed in a special case which we pass around. We hold our hands up to the bright flame and bless God, the light of the fire, for making distinctions between Holy and ordinary, light and darkness, and Shabbos and weekday. We then drink from the cup of wine and douse the candle with a few drops of wine.

Standing in the darkness, arms around each other, we sing *Shavuah Tov*, a song wishing each other a good week, and Eliyahu HaNavi, a prayer for the coming of Elijah the Prophet, who is expected to precede the appearance of the Messiah.

The lights are turned on — we play dance music on the stereo — the phone is connected and starts ringing — we listen to the messages that have come in . . .

The week has begun.

■　　■　　■

## Moon Work: Attunement to the Flow

To build a cohesive communal structure it is necessary to orient community events around the monthly turning of the moon. The turning of the moon effects the deepest strata of the psyche. During patriarchal periods of dominance the moon is always eclipsed. In male ruled societies the pulse of life inevitably falls out of alignment with the procreative pulse of nature. We are currently in the process of emerging from a two thousand year reign of moon ignorance. Contemporary women are often as mystified by their ovulatory/menstrual cycles as men are of their seed.

Just the other day I heard a woman doctor arguing in favor of estrogen replacement therapy (for middle-aged women). She said that until very recently hardly any women lived long enough to experience menopause. She claimed mother nature just didn't know how to cope! Oh, how comprehensive the brainwashing! For thousands and thousands of years women have successfully entered their non-fertile years. Such ideology is indicative of just how far we have strayed from that long-ago cast-off part of ourselves, the moon.

We all have the dynamics of a waxing and waning moon within our bodies. We all come from a womb whose tides are controlled by the ebb and flow of a Heavenly Body. The moon actually flows within our bodies. The flow and ebb of emotion and physiological cycles are influenced by the tides. Women ovulate and menstruate with the moon. This is true for men as well as for women. Both men and women are moon-attuned. The moon turns in male blood, too. The male body bleeds, but his blood is hidden from view. Men also shed a part of themselves each month to make room for new life. Oftentimes extreme horniness is a sign that a man is "mooning".

The moon's effect on the tides influences both the seed sacks of the male and the ovaries and womb of the female. There is a vital "pull" on each gender's physical body. There is a vital interchange between earth and water within each of us. For both men and women the moon stirs emotions. Our emotions are the most changing part of our nature. Each of the moon's phases has distinct forces and counter forces to which we are all vulnerable.

Acknowledging this vulnerability can be of tremendous help to couples. When a couple celebrates the cycles of the moon, they are better able to communicate. One way to celebrate is to "moon fast" together, eating lightly or fasting completely during a specific phase of the moon, which ideally would coincide with menstruation. Fasting or eating lightly during menstruation assists the natural cleansing that occurs at the time.

*The following recipes are formulated to meet the specific nutritional needs of menstruation and, at the same time, to effect a more powerful menstrual cleansing:*

## ROOT RECIPE

Boil for 12 minutes:
One part dandelion (iron)
Two parts burdock (phosphorus)
1/8 part angelica (potassium)

Steep for 12 minutes
One part peppermint (digestive aid)
Fenugreek seed (iron, $B_{17}$ compounds)
Chamomile (calcium)

Tea may be mixed with
One part fresh (raw) goat's milk (lactose minerals)
One part pollen (nucleic acid balance)
Nutritional yeast (complete B complex)
Honey ($B_{12}$, manganese, and carbohydrate)

## NUTRI-SOUP

Miso broth base
whole grain (brown rice or other whole grain)
shitake mushrooms (optional*)
beans, dry or fresh
vegetables (in season)
seaweed
Fo-ti-teng (Chinese herb)

drink the liquid and eat only small amounts of the solid ingredients

"Fasting" on such a soup is safe and nutritionally sound as well as assisting cleansing especially during menstruation.

* Shitake mushrooms are excellent intestinal and genital regenerators

## SALAD #1

Grate: raw beet, carrot
Add: parsley, ground sunlower seeds, chia seeds, flax meal

## SALAD #2

Fresh fruit (in season)
top with yogurt, alfalfa sprouts, and local bee pollen

Juices are also excellent, two mixtures being especially helpful:

1) Carrot-beet juice with spinach, parsley, and celery

2) A fresh fruit juice blend of grapefruit, grape, apple, pineapple, and papaya, diluted with water.

*Oceanic Recipe*: create tea/broth mixtures containing any/all of the following:

Seaweed (contains all known minerals)
Nettles (sodium)
Carrot, beet, celery, parsley, winter or summer squash
Winter melon (in season)
Miso (friendly bacteria, protein)

Another important area to focus on during times of menstruation is healing one's relationship with parents. The foundation of our way of relating was established in childhood; was affected by our birthing, bonding, infancy, and early, as well as later, rapport with our parents. The dynamics acted out in our intimate relationships are a reflection of early patterns of relating to parents. This is especially prominent once we take on the role and responsibilities of being parents ourselves. If we want to create new, more positive healing dynamics in our inter-relationships. It is always helpful to "clean the slate" as much as possible, and release past patterns. The following exercise provides an affirmation of liberation.

## Allowing the Blood to Purify Us

First, imagine: Being unborn . . . Being a drop in the ocean, a fish in the sea. Be a bird in flight, a redwood tree.

After feeling the expansiveness of these forms of being, imagine the moment of your conception.

In your mind's eye, see your parents entwined in joyous ecstasy. Feel the holiness of their union.

As you feel your conception, let the fullness of Love fill you.

Now: With your parents clearly in your heart, make a place for them in this five-pointed prayer of forgiveness and regeneration.

Step one: In your mind's eye, place your parents on a prayer altar.

Step two: Say "Thank you, mother."

Step three: Say "Thank you, father."

Step four: Feel deep gratitude in your heart that they conceived you. Feel forgiveness for any unconscious suffering which they may have caused you or you may have caused them.

Step five: Now, be born anew. Feel the Divine One who Always Lives in the Temple of your Womb.

Michael Markowitz

## Moon Celebrations

Celebration of the flowing moon brings community together. The moon is our common ground. Our dreaming mass of energy which hovers near our earth. Indeed, the moon is a part of the earth. Attunement to the moon is necessary to complete the human psyche. It is the moon that weds the Sun and Earth. The moon regulates the cyclic force of Creation. The lunar body enlightens the Presence in the womb. It is the light that signals our bodies to conceive, bleed, dance, and seek solitude. Let us share this rhythm with each other as we celebrate the flowing changes of the moon.

It is helpful to gather with trusted friends during all the phases of the moon.

## Dark of Moon

The dark of the moon is the time of the month when the fear of death is greatest. During this three or four day period, we are more involved with the subtler working of the intellect. Thought tends to weave in the mystical mode and there is an increased awareness of the transitory aspect of being, of the breathing and pulsating of mortality. To whatever degree, and in whatever form the fear of death resides in us, we are most vulnerable to its influence during the dark of the moon.

We must be prepared for its periodic confrontation with our subconscious reality. We must make an effort to illuminate the darkness with the light of consciousness. THE DARK OF THE-MOON IS THE MOST AUSPICIOUS TIME FOR US TO WORK ON HEALING OUR FEAR OF DEATH. The moon teaches us, in her constant returning, that the flow of life is eternal.

## New Moon

During the new moon mental clarity is especially lucid. There is a fertility of mind which is conducive to planting new ideas. The new moon tunes up the mind. When you gather with the new moon, affirm your intentions. Let us focus our intention on our family and friends. Appreciate what is truly before us. Focus love by serving those with whom you live, work, and study. So often we keep love feelings inside. On the new moon, let us affirm our intention to express our feelings of love, and serve those who are vulnerable. Let us make a vow to share our love.

## Full Moon

The full moon provides an optimal time for reflection. The fullness of the moon reflects the fullness of life. During this time, our physical bodies want to eat, drink, and be sexual. However, remember, no hunger can be satisifed during the full moon. This is not the time of the month to satisfy hunger. This the time to be attuned to that which is hungry and to be filled by Light. Dance, sing, and rejoice. Join together in celebration. Stay up all night and pray for guidance.

Myrica's Mooning Song

*Full moon finds me*
*reaching out for my sisters*
*Kiss the Earth*
*which sustains us*
*Feel the pulse of life*
*in her breast*
*This blood I release*
*is for the suffering*
*of the earth*
*Gather together, sisters*
*Let us sing in a circle*
*the circle that empowers us*
*the circle that heals*
*Claim your right*
*I am a woman*
*pure light reflecting*
*Strong and pure and giving*
*nourishing, protecting*
*Sisters, come and join me*
*Sing of our powers*

## Receiving the Light: Meeting to Pray

The Earth goes through Four distinct phases in her path around the Sun. The year is a circle. The flight of the Earth around the Sun is an outer expression of an innate symmetry that exists in the psyche. The rotation of the Earth around the Sun happens inside the Body. Changing light affects every cell in the Body. It is this way from the very beginning of Life. The child first feels the magnetic pull of light while floating inside the water of the Womb. Floating in her waters we feel the waxing and waning of the moon. We actually feel the moon through her skin. We subtly turn around inside of her in order to get a better angle of light. Light enraptures us while we grow in the blisswaters.

Once outside, the human needs full-spectrum light in the right amounts and at appropriate times of the day. When this does not occur, the result is "malillumination." John Ott, the foremost authority on the effects of light, coined this term to describe the ill effects that occur when our exposure to full-spectrum light is blocked by glasses, windows, and layers of smog. Ott's research has verified that most civilized people do not receive enough light in the retina of the eyes to catalyze key physiological processes.

Dr. Ray Gottlieb is a friend of mine and an associate of John Ott's. He is an optometrist and a psychologist with an extensive clinical practice in light therapy. I asked him about light. He responded:

Science knows for certain that there are nerve pathways that start at the eye with light stimulation and end up on those brain areas that are most basic for the balancing of our body fuctions. These are the brain areas that regulate our glands, enzymes, and chemistry to prepare us for changes in the environment due to seasonal changes of summer, spring, and so. They also control our sexuality, hunger, thirst, how much urine we secrete, *water levels* contained inside and outside our cells, how much *energy* is to be used or stored, how sensitive we are to pain, light, etc.

Animals function very much according to the seasons. Sheep ovulate only at a certain time of the year. Animal hair, including ours, grows fastest at certain times, fat is deposited differently, certain moods of aggression, migration, hibernation, feather moulting, and other behaviors happen only at certain times of the year.

*The stimulant for these changes is light.* The amount of light changes in Earth's yearly trip around the sun and so does the color of the light. The length of the red tinted sunset and twilight, the redness of the dawn, and the overall color of daylight change with the seasons. These variations in light stimulate animals (plants are even more obvious in their responses to light) to prepare, in advance, for seasonal changes in temperature and humidity.

Other evidence about light comes from examining how the body gets and stores energy from our food. *All of the energy which the body needs* in order to move and pump and think *is created by light.* Energy from sunlight is absorbed by sensitive pigments in plants. This light energy is stored in the chemical bonding of certain molecules in the plant. When we eat these plants their stored energy is absorbed into the blood stream and is converted into energy forms for use in our body. If we eat an animal, all the energy we get from that animal came from the stored sunlight in the vegetation which it had eaten. In fact, the whole system which converts the digested energy from the plants we eat, stores that energy in our fat and protein storage areas, or converts it directly into glycogen for our immediate use, seems to be driven and controlled by light. If this system of energy evolved through light, it is reasonable to suspect that it can be influenced by light even in our complex system of digestion and energy transfer.

■　　■　　■

Though light affects the Human organism exactly as it affects all other forms of life there is something unique about the Human. The Human Being has to pray before receiving. The Children of Earth must pray in order for there to be balance and harmony. We no longer live a Garden where we may roam in innocence. We have the capacity to be free, but we must pray first. Prayer insures freedom.

The Children of Earth have the capacity to Be Free. We contain all the knowledge necessary. We are born with it. All Human Beings are born with the innate capacity to be happy and creative. But S/he must learn to pray before Creation can be actualized. Prayer is the water that nurtures the Tree. Before eating of the Tree the Human must bend down and pray. The Earth grows the Tree. The work of the Human is to eat. The food of earth is made sweet by prayer. Prayer ripens the fruit. Prayer sends light to the world and cultivates the soil of truth. Prayer cleanses the body and releases the limited self from exile. Prayer generates the will forward, prayer is the Exodus. Prayer is the only force on earth that can get the Children to the other side. In the Free World the children exercise their right to pray. In the Free World the Children gather together in Circles of Love and generate their will forward with the turning of the Sun.

The Solstices and Equinoxes are special times to pray and meet. They are times to get together with your loved ones beneath the Great Canopy of the Sky. Meet by rivers, at the mouths of oceans, on mountains, on the deserts and plains. Meet wherever you are. Call up your friends and bring your drums and rattles. Bring special feathers, crystals, turquoise. Wrap up your gifts in a little bundle. Bring along a poem or a dream. Bring your dreams along. Gather together to build community.

Gather together in Circles of Unity. To be free you must love and to love you must belong to a circle of friends. Friends are essential to prayer. There is something Divine when ten or more gather to praise the One. Wherever you gather is Holy. Gather in parks and on street corners. Prayer determines place. Of course the prayers will change with the tone of each particular season. The way you will sing in Spring is unique to Spring.

Spring is the natural mating time of the year. When the First Wedding Ceremony takes place. In the Free World the Children are allowed to mate and have children at any age they choose. Babies are ushered into the Circle. Our Prayer Meetings are open to the youngest amongst us. This is how we defend our freedom. We acknowledge before our Children that we are grateful to the Divine Beloved for sending them to us. Spring is the most fertile season. Just like ovulation, it is over very quickly. Spring seems to pass the quickest. Most of the year is spent building the egg. By the time June 21 rolls around the light will begin to fade.

During the Spring/Summer transition it is especially important to be conscious of one's sexuality. This is the time of the year to check genital health. Men should feel around their penis and testicles. They should also pay attention to diet, emotional blockage and how they feel first thing in the morning. If there is any sign of distrubance the Spring is the perfect time to begin a meditation schedule, yoga practice, Tai-Chi workout, or a Dance class.

Women should check their menstrual blood and gauge their emotional response to their ovulatory cycle. If there is any cramping or conflict it is the perfect time of the year to change the timing of your flow. If you bleed on the new moon, shift your tides to the full. Ovulate on the New Moon. By utilizing the Light of the Summer Solstice you can change the cycling of your tides. Just visualize it so, standing naked in the full light of the sun.

Jeffrey Kaus

If there is any question about the general vitality of your reproductive organs, Spring/Summer is the time to seek help. And then do not get "checked" again until the following Spring. Give yourself time to heal. If you live in accordance with Nature your body will do everything within its power to heal you. Trust now. Spring is the Time of the year to trust. It is the time of the year when it is appropriate to trust beyond the limits of your imagination. To stretch out. Spring and Summer are a time for expanision.

The Light cycle of the year is the time to bond families together and widen the support system. Now is the time for the son and daughter who has never seen their father to cry out to him. This is the time of the year to find God-Parents for your Children. Every child should have God-parents. Every child deserves to be connected to a large famiy that transcends blood lines.

In the Fall, the Light fades, it is time to seek out the Source of Light. Time to go inside again. To get naked before the altar. To meet the Maker. To forgive and let go of any anger you may be holding toward someone. To let go of the toxic accumulations of the past. As the Light fades it is a perfect time to fast for a few days. It is the time to get down on one's knees and touch one's head to the ground. To be grateful for what is. Exactly as it is.

There is no time for distraction in the Fall. There is too much to do to get ready to meet the Darkness with a clear Heart and a healthy body. In the Fall we must Remember the Ones who came before us. It is the time to let the tears flow forth from your eyes. This is how you can tell the Seekers. Freedom is earned through tears. A Free people cry out and wail. In the light. They will cry out when they see injustice. Freedom does not come easy. It is not for sale. It cannot be bartered or taken away. As the Dark cycle of the year approaches it is time to Return to the Source. Freedom is found near the salty water.

This is the Way of Life. In the Darkest Hour the Sun Returns. Happens every time. Always has been that way. Always will be that way. For as long as the Earth does spin. After the rains, come the flowers. All of us are Love-Children living in the Promised Land. All of us are Children of the Dawn.

# CIRCLE OF LOVE

The Ancient One Gives Way
All the Children Are Called
The New Born is Washed Clean
By The Empty Belly of Creation
O' Sun Return
Enter Us
On the Wings Of Your Drum
Bring All The Nations
Into The Circle Of Love

We are birthed
with prayers and chants
We are spirit
with bodies divine
We are of mother and father
We are of earth
as the sun rises
We are ready
to dance with creation

## Song For The Road
## O' Beloved Ones

Every nation shall be your home and you shall find friends wherever you go. You belong to a Family that includes all nations. You are a Free People, Walking on the Road of Life. The old order is over. You have been born in the Promised Land. You have been born to walk this Way. You are the Peace-Makers and the Builders of the new foundation.

You must join your families into great circles of families. You must get organized and prepare yourselves for the changes that are coming. By the year 2000 the whole planet must be Free. All the nations must come into the circle. This is why you were born and will continue to be born.

By the year 2000 the people will sing in harmony and speak the language of the Heart. The Sound of Life will be heard all over the Land. The Sound will be heard from shore to shore. People of the mountains will hear the Sound and People of the plains will hear the Sound. The Sound of Life will cause the workers to stop and give praise. Students will set their books down. Mothers and Fathers, with children by their sides, will look in the same direction.

By the year 2000 there will be midwives present at the President's birth. And the voice of the mother will be heard in the halls of congress. The White House will be turned into a Light House. Rays of Light will emanate from Washington. A national crusade to save the environment will be initiated. The rivers will be cleansed of their pollution. The toxic agricultural fields will be put to fallow. The oceans will be declared off limits to the military industrial complex. Everything will turn toward Life. . . .

Have faith, Children. The Road is long but you must keep on walking. The Ancestors have walked before you. The Road has been scouted out. You will be protected. There is a great and fertile valley awaiting around the next bend. Keep on walking. One step at a time. One breath at a time. One life time at a time.

You are the Children of the Dawn and you have the collective power to fulfill the destiny of your nation. Seek out the ways of your Grandmothers. Listen to her calling. Go home to the mouths of rivers. Lay down your sword. Raise up your hands in a mighty gesture of Love. Truly, the Road is good and you will receive guidance from the center.

The Way is clear. All that you do now enters into the covenant of the New World. You are the Children of the Dawn. The Lord of Creation is the early morning Light. You will make your way back to this soil and know right where to plant your foot on the Path.

# ACKNOWLEDGMENTS

Sandra Boucher, Melinda McKown, Radha Malasquez, Wendy Sherman, Susan Barnes, Sahedran Sattizahn, who read and typed the manuscript; Reuben Halpern, my editor; Daniel Pinney, Rosemary Gladstar, Michael Tierra, for their work in the healing arts; Manu and Ethan for Rainbow trail drumming; Malcolm Margolin for patient advice; Sedonia Cahill, beloved co-worker; the dancing Goddess of Big Sur, for sharing the secret of the canyons; backcover photo credit, Sarah Dovbish.

Special thanks to artists Donna Chess (Saturn Raine), illustrations on pages 2, 22, 36, 48, 80, 104, 132, 158. Brian McGovern, illustrations on pages 5, 38, 109, 169. Gray Shephard, illustrations on pages XV, XVII, XIX, XXI, 3, 23, 37, 49, 81, 105, 133, 159 and Robin Shivani Brunn, illustrations on pages I, 47, 131 for working closely with me in the creative process.

Note to the Reader: If this book has been significant for you, please let your friends know. Word of mouth is the best mode of travel. Also, if you would like to share your stories, notify OWL PUBLICATIONS.
I Love You, Joshua

# INDEX

# Children of the Dawn

About the Author:

Joshua Halpern was born and raised in Northern California. At fourteen he attended John Woolman School, a Quaker boarding school in the Sierra Nevadas. After high school he joined with friends in forming a spiritual community and began studying Oriental medicine. In 1968 he founded the first vegetarian restaurant in Berkeley, California. In 1975 he received a masters degree in community psychology and a doctorate in natural healing. In 1980 his first book, Live your Health, co-authored with his father, was published. His third book, Circling the Boundaries of Earth, will be published in the Spring of 1988.

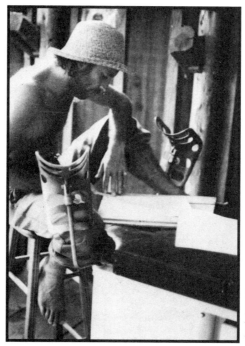

davidburns